networking for global impact

LINCOLN CHRISTIAN COLLEGE AND SEMINARY

ministry

The Next Step: North American Partnership of Mission Trainers is equipping Christian workers for effective cross-cultural ministry.

The Next Step's online mission training database and regional/national network of mission trainers is helping people develop their ministry skills, as well as, prepare them for the challenges of living abroad.

For information about mission training opportunities, the benefits of Next Step membership and member initiatives, please visit our website.

www.thenextstep.org

THE NEXT STEP
North American Partnership in Mission Training

CONNECTING, COMMUNICATING AND COOPERATING IN MISSION TRAINING

Crisis
War
Disaster
Famine
Tornado
Flood
Drought
Disease

2000 years ago, Jesus preached the Gospel, healed the sick and fed the hungry.

Do we dare do anything less today?

Put your compassion to work.

Contact:

WORLD RELIEF
www.worldrelief.org
e-mail: wr@xc.org
1-800-535-LIFE

Frontiers

A MISSION AGENCY DEDICATED TO REACHING THE MUSLIM WORLD.

ALLAHU AKBAR!

5 Times A Day Muslims Hear This - "GOD IS GREAT!" Will you be the first to tell them "GOD IS LOVE"?

How many missionaries has your church sent out in the last year?

10
9
8
7
6
5
4
3
2
1
0

Acts 13:1-5

..a strategy to raise up and send 200,000 new missionaries to the harvest field in obedience to the command of Jesus Christ (Matthew 28:19).

Your church can make a vital difference! Join the ACTS 13 - Breakthrough initiative.

We have a range of free resources to help you get involved.

Contact: AD2000 Missions Mobilization Network
PO Box 660, London SE23 3ST, England.
Tel:44 (0) 181-699-6077 Email:chacko.thomas@l.ict.om.or

ACTS 13 BREAKTHROUGH

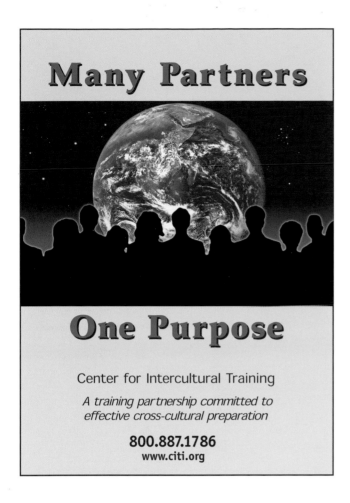
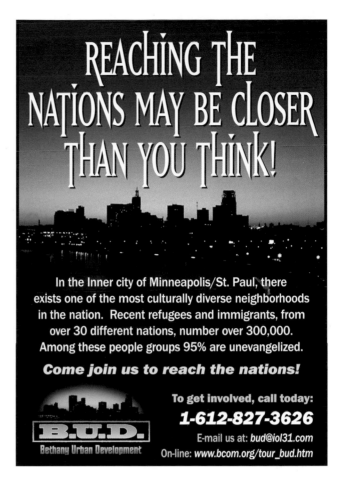

ACMC

Advancing Churches in Missions Commitment

ACMC helps **churches mobilize** their resources **for effective** involvement in **world evangelization**

Training

Resources

Consulting

To find out more about the ACMC network of churches visit our web site at *www.acmc.org* or call *800.747.7346*

Send Me!

Your Journey to the Nations

STEVE HOKE
&
BILL TAYLOR

Copyright © 1999
World Evangelical Fellowship
Missions Commission
All rights reserved

Co-published by:
World Evangelical Fellowship Missions Commission and
William Carey Library

For additional copies, please contact:
**Distribution Central, PO Box 40519,
Pasadena, CA 91114. (626) 798-8582.**
$8 for a single copy. 10+ copies--$7 each.
25+ copies--$6 each. 100+ copies--$5 each.
ISBN 0-87808-294-8

Printed in the United States of America

Order more books from:
www.wefbookstore.org

Acknowledgments

You Can So Get There From Here was originally published by MARC in 1969 and was reprinted through 1991. Revised by Steve Hoke and Bill Taylor as *Send Me! Your Journey to the Nations*, by permission of MARC/World Vision International, 800 W. Chestnut, Monrovia, CA 91016-3198.

Permission to reprint material was granted by the following publishers:

- *Wherever* magazine, published by TEAM, P.O. Box 969, Wheaton, IL 60189-0969.

- *Perspective*, *Focus*, and *Mentoring* workbooks by Terry Walling. Carol Stream, IL: CRM Publishers/Church-Smart Resources, 1996. Phone: 1-800-253-4276.

- Public Relations, Columbia International University, P.O. Box 3122, Columbia, SC 29230-3122.

- *Missions Today*, *The Short-Term Mission Handbook*, and *The Great Commission Handbook*. Berry Publishing, 701 Main St., Evanston, IL 60202.

Scripture quotations are taken from the Holy Bible, New International Version. Copyright © 1973, 1978, 1984 by the International Bible Society. Used by permission of Zondervan Publishing House, Grand Rapids, MI 49506. All rights reserved.

Technical editors: Matthew Hoffman, Susan Peterson
Cover design: Omer Mahmud, Kerry Lammi

Dedication

To Don and Martha Hoke,

my missionary parents,

whose appropriate nurture

and unfailing encouragement

have guided

my own journey

to the nations

for the last 40 years.

~ *Steve Hoke* ~

To Bill and Stella Taylor,

my own missionary parents,

with deepest respect

for their example as

lifelong servant leaders,

long-term cross-cultural

veterans, and

still-living models.

~ *Bill Taylor* ~

And to the generation

that will follow us—

gifted and committed

radicals

who will serve as

global citizens

with a passion

to pack heaven

with worshipers!

ABOUT THE AUTHORS

Steve Hoke

Vice President of Training
Church Resource Ministries

Growing up as a missionary kid in Tokyo, Japan, I very early committed to lifelong involvement in world evangelization. I wanted to be a part of what God was doing around the world! It just took me a while to find the niche God had carved out for me. Through college, several church ministries, and grad school, I realized my gifting was not as an evangelist, but as an encourager and teacher. In serving as a missions prof and director of campus ministries at Seattle Pacific University, director of field training for World Vision International, president of LIFE Ministries (Japan), and presently as vice president of training of Church Resource Ministries (CRM), my gift mix has been confirmed. I'm a Barnabas, not a barnstorming church planter like Paul.

In my present role, I help mobilize, train, and encourage international teams for ministry around the world. I visit over a dozen churches each year to advise and encourage them in their mission ministry, and I mentor several young missions pastors. I also work with groups like ACMC (Advancing Churches in Missions Commitment) to equip churches nationwide in global ministries. My passion in the years ahead is to help raise up the next generation of mission leaders from churches across North America and the world, and to see that they are effective in their roles as intercultural servant-leaders.

I've been married to Eloise since 1972. Our daughter Stephenie is in college, and our son Chris is a senior in high school. We've lived in southern California since 1985.

Bill Taylor

Executive Director
Missions Commission
World Evangelical Fellowship

I'm a "Third Culture Person" who was born in Costa Rica, and lived 30 years in Latin America. My parents moved to the U.S. for my last year of high school. I returned with my artist wife, Yvonne, to work in Central America after too many years of college and seminary study! A Ph.D. in Latin American studies from the University of Texas, Austin, came later. A former Texas staff of InterVarsity Christian Fellowship, I served 17 years with CAM International in leadership development at the Seminario Teológico Centroamericano in Guatemala. Yvonne and I were also on a church planting team in Guatemala for a church supporting us today as one of their international missionary families.

Based in Austin, Texas, I serve the global missions force through WEF in missiological concerns, developing national missionary movements, missionary training, strategic research, and publications.

Married for 32 years, Yvonne and I have served all these years in cross-cultural missions. Hope Chapel is our Austin church. Our three "twenty-something" kids (two single, one married) were all born during our years in Guatemala. My passions: to finish well and to do all I can to pack heaven with worshipers.

c o n t

e n t s

Grounding the Next Steps: A Personal Fitness Assessment

GROUNDING THE NEXT STEPS: A PERSONAL FITNESS ASSESSMENT

Steve Hoke

Like high altitude mountain climbing, short-term or long-term mission takes careful planning and preparation. If you "train" right and "pack" well, you'll be ready to handle the unexpected and weather the difficulties. Before you get started, here's a "mini-personal fitness assessment" program with three levels—self-awareness, sensitivity, and practical skills. Greater self-awareness will lead to greater sensitivity, which, in turn, will help you develop greater practical ministry skills.

> *Greater self-awareness will lead to greater sensitivity, which, in turn, will help you develop greater practical ministry skills.*

Self-awareness level. You'll carry your culture with you—whether you're conscious of it or not. Self-awareness begins with a clearer understanding of yourself. Until you see yourself as you really are, you'll see others from a distorted point of view. The first part of your personal preparation program helps you gain a balanced perspective with the use of two very simple tools.

Taking a cross-sectional view: Profile of a critical role needed today. The first self-assessment tool allows you to see how *who* you are today matches with the profile of a critical role needed in missions today, that of a cross-cultural church planter. This is only one of a variety of important missionary roles needed today, including the Bible translator, the provider of technical services, the mentor-coach, and the tentmaker. Some of the new roles include serving as facilitators, along-side trainers, leader developers, and side-by-side encouragers. But we've chosen this role as a baseline profile because it takes into account some of the most important personal character traits, ministry skills, and knowledge areas you will need to have.

Evaluating your readiness. The second self-assessment tool asks a series of questions as you read through the case study of two actual couples as they prepared their next steps into missions. Their stories and the issues raised may give you a framework from which to see the importance of evaluating your own readiness at this time.

Journal worksheet: How do I shape up for missions? The third self-assessment tool is a journal worksheet asking guiding questions for you to think and pray about in all three related areas—self-awareness, sensitivity, and practical skills. Jotting down your honest assessment of where you see yourself now will serve as a helpful benchmark as you continue to grow spiritually, mentally, and relationally.

The better job you do of self-evaluation at this initial phase, the better you will be prepared to respond honestly and thoughtfully to the questions of others as you take your first steps into missions involvement. You'll be packed and ready to go. You'll have a sense of, "Hey, I've already thought and prayed about that. I'm ready to take the next step."

THE BIG PICTURE: IT'S RISKY BUSINESS CHARTING YOUR JOURNEY TO THE NATIONS

Steve Hoke and Bill Taylor

Living in a context of constant change can be both exhilarating and disturbing. Thrilling because it is constantly shifting and presenting you new options and experiences. Uneasy because the swirl of life and history at times seems too random. Life is chaotic much of the time!

In the global mission enterprise, we experience all varieties and degrees of emotions and conditions. Just consider some of the realities you and I face as citizens of our world at this unique historical hinge—we will soon enter a new century and a new millennium, for better or for worse.

Macro Issues Facing Us In Our Interlinked World Community

• Constant political change presents fresh daily challenges to political and Christian leadership.

• Unending tensions and violence between ethnic groups and religious factions make you wonder where tribalism will take us.

• An historic migratory mobilization of the peoples is taking place due to shifting economics and political violence. Result? The nations are everywhere!

• New and sophisticated terrorism threatens our civilization—no one is safe anywhere!

• Apparently random natural physical disasters unleash uncontrollable chaos.

• Economic crises in one region inevitably ripple around the world, impacting the global family, all linked to the borderless economy.

• Resurgent world religions (some not previously considered missionary) are on the march, with attractive adaptations to "win the West."

• Populations explode and cluster most clearly in the cities—whether small or mega-world class in size.

• Christians around the globe constantly grapple with endemic injustice, disproportionate wealth distribution, and poverty, and they wonder, "What can I do?"

• The post-modern world is with us—with all of its implications at the level of lifestyle, arts and literature, science and technology, spirituality and religion.

From this hemispheric perspective, we look inwards, evaluating the status of the Christian faith, its various communities and its missionary movement. Each region and/or country has its own particularities, so let us focus only on North America, with possible application to Europe.

Macro Issues Facing Our Christian Community in the West

• The anemic, fractured church in the West is now recognizing that something is lacking and that it needs a new, radical openness to the Spirit of God. May it gain a heart that listens to and learns from the church in Asia, Latin America, Africa, the Middle East, and the island nations.

• There is a growing sense that God is at work in history, and not just because of the historical hinge just before us. We may well be entering the last major phase of history. Think of what might happen if the global church were to live in holiness and in the power of the Spirit of God. Radical faith communities would extend into every locale, reaching out to the disenfranchised and investing their highest resources to establish these faith-in-Christ communities wherever they do not yet exist. If the church were truly to live locally its passion as the redeemed fellowship, this would inevitably spill over into the entire world.

We live in a season of major transitions, as a friend has said, "entering a change-over season from the days of Moses to the days of Joshua." What might that mean? We don't know for sure. But we do see a number of crucial changes:

• Creativity, responsibility, and authority are being transferred from the older to the younger Christian generation.

• A new wave of younger leaders has emerged—leaders who passionately desire to live as practicing supernaturalists in a secular world and who are willing to play a high-risk game of radically following Jesus. These are creatively starting new Christian ventures in the name of Jesus.

> *Think of what might happen if the global church were to live in holiness and in the power of the Spirit of God.*

• The tectonic shift of Christianity from the North to both South and East teaches us that the Spirit is moving—without abandoning the North.

• The nations of the world have come to the West, with great opportunity to tell them the Great Story of Christ. It is also a chance for Western churches to be infected with the family and celebratory values of these younger Christian communities now implanted in the West.

- Ownership of the missions movement has shifted from the parachurch groups to partnerships with local churches—with greater church involvement in selection, screening, testing, equipping, supporting, interceding, strategizing, and shepherding of the mission force. There is also a call for church partnerships with training schools and field based agencies.

- There has been an explosion of short-term missions as significant appetizers of cross-cultural reality and ministry for thousands of young and older adults, some of whom will be forever changed, and others who will return to invest longer seasons of their life in mission.

- Missions language and definitions are being reworked, allowing greater geographical mobility, a broader flexibility of vocational change during a lifetime, more focus on teams, and sequential terms of service with longer periods at "home" for ministry, equipping, restoration, and then returning to cross-cultural work.

This may very well be the generation that will witness the greatest spiritual harvest of history—but it will not come easily. Be prepared to serve and suffer in ways you may not imagine.

- The skill sets and gift mixes needed for ministry in "open" as well as "restricted access" nations present unique challenges, as does the need for high originality to develop new "creative access platforms" for longer-term ministry.

- We must avoid oversimplifications (reductionism) of complex missions realities. The Great Commission is more than just evangelization. The unreached world is vaster than the 10/40 Window. "People group" thinking is only one paradigm of need reality. Short terms are great, but they aren't a substitute for the longer-term cross-cultural servant.

- Our next generation of Western missionaries must go out as servants, able to serve alongside and under leadership from other cultures and mother languages.

Making the Connection

So there you have it! This is our own limited reading on history and our role in God's Story. Thank God that His Story is going somewhere, and so is your life. But we must take the time to make the connections between events and trends that some observers might describe as random. Do you resonate with a desire (even a passion) to impact the nations for Christ, but perhaps feel as if you are exploring uncharted territories?

This interactive workbook is a tool to help you make sense of the data that flood you. It will coach you in making connections between your experience and interests, world events, and God's global plan for all people. It will do these things in a way that will help you draw your own course on a complicated map. That's why we call it *Send Me! Your Journey to the Nations*.

Ultimately, no one else but you and the sovereign Lord can draw the connections. In a sense, you have the steering wheel in your hands—empowered by the Spirit, counseled by God's people, and grounded in your values and commitments. But the wisdom of others' experiences and knowing the story of how the church has gotten to this point may assist you in your own journey. For these reasons, you'll want to work with others in this project. It's in community that God today truly wants to reveal Himself. We need one another. Invite your community of friends, family, spouse, spiritual leaders, veteran missionaries, and cross-cultural workers into the planning process.

Come! Let us walk this lifelong, global pilgrimage of strong obedience together. Let us experience both the pain of our world as well as the thrill of what God is doing and is about to do to redeem the nations. This may very well be the generation that will witness the greatest spiritual harvest of history—but it will not come easily. Be prepared to serve and suffer in ways you may not imagine. Thousands have gone before, and thousands will accompany you in this cross-cultural pilgrimage. They come from Africa, Asia, Latin America, the Caribbean, the Middle East, and the South Pacific. They journey to the nations who are without a witness to Christ's power and glory. The next generation of redemptive history belongs to these holy ambassadors of the Most High God!

PARTICIPATE IN THE STORY OF HIS GLORY

Bill Taylor

It's an experience forever engraved upon my memory. We were standing under a large tent pitched just outside Auckland, New Zealand, during one of the evening sessions of the South Pacific Prayer Assembly. My wife, Yvonne, and I were privileged to join believers from eight South Pacific nations for this week-long event. The worship had been rich, the prayer powerful, the diversity of peoples, languages, cultures, and interdenominational streams of Christian faith simply glorious. That night, God led Michael Maelieu of the Solomon Islands to preside over the meeting in a special way. He told stories of God's work in the islands, thanking the Westerners present for bringing the gospel to their isolated region and paying the high cost of their very lives. He shared the story of the dramatic advance of the gospel among his people—people who 100 years ago were an unreached, cannibal people group.

But then Michael's focus changed. "Now we island believers have heard God calling us to share with you, our Australian and New Zealand brothers and sisters, the flaming missionary torch of the gospel you so lovingly brought to us." He called all the Papua New Guinea and Solomon islanders up to the front, then the Aussie and Kiwi leaders. Then he challenged his island peoples to encircle and minister to their Western colleagues. The heavenly-sounding cacophony of prayer, singing, weeping, and worship was incredible. Islanders were praying for Australians and New Zealanders. The former mission fields had been converted into new prayer and sending bases for world evangelization. We sensed deeply that the transactions taking place that evening would transform history in that region.

Flash Forward to Heaven!

In my mind I was transported to that majestic series of 17 worship scenarios that play out in the drama of the book of Revelation. In chapters 4–7, John the apostle, pastor, poet, and prophet offers us seven glorious multimedia scenes which center attention on our unique, living God and His Lamb. These scenes range from the four mysterious creatures to the 24 elders, from the angels to all creation, and from these choirs to that unprecedented worship procession where John writes:

"After this I looked and there before me was *a great multitude that no one could count, from every nation, tribe, people, and language*, standing before the throne and in front of the Lamb. They were wearing white robes and were holding palm branches in their hands. And they cried out in a loud voice: 'Salvation belongs to our God, who sits on the throne, and to the Lamb'" (Rev. 7:9-10).

Now, how did all those peoples get there? The story of God's glory begins with God's passionate heart for all His creation, for people made in His image who are loved in spite of their rebellion. Furthermore, children, youth, and adults have sensed the deep conviction that God is asking them to leave their own culture and family in order to cross cultural, language, and geographic barriers to present the claims of our unique Christ and establish His church among these different peoples. And these people have been willing to pay the price. Their obedience has been costly; to leave home to serve in another context is never easy. There are plenty of tough times, bitter and sweet tears, gut-wrenching pain and loss, darkness and despair. Satan does not relinquish his captives easily! But these servants persevere for the sake of the Lamb who is worthy to receive all praise and worship.

The Importance of Worship

The prime and ultimate business of heaven is worship. Pastor John Piper puts it bluntly: "Missions is not the ultimate goal of the church. Worship is." So why do we still have missions? "Missions exists," Piper reminds us, "because worship doesn't." The task of claiming worshipers for God and His Lamb is unfinished business. Thus, worship and mission merge as my overarching passions, for I want to pack heaven with worshipers.

At the end of the 20th century, and as we move into the third millennium, the church of Jesus Christ has become truly globalized, and missions is now *from* all nations *to* all nations. We stand at an incredibly significant crossroads. This is a *kairos* moment, and we're privileged to be a part of it. Thousands of faithful disciples have preceded us and participated in the harvest.

But in order to see heaven packed with the final ingathering of worshipers from all the nations, we need a strong, new, international army of long-term, cross-cultural workers. We must deploy a new generation of cross-cultural workers who will live in the slums, identify with the oppressed, the widows and orphans, who will cry out for justice! They and their colleagues in other ministries will be ones who will commit to stay long enough to learn the language well, to understand the culture, and to love the people, and thus incarnate the gospel and see the church established. They are the ones who will have the inexpressible joy of seeing those whom they served join the vast multitudes already surrounding the throne of God and worshiping the Lamb.

We will have the privilege of presenting the once-unreached peoples to our Lord as our offering of praise. That's where history is going, and that's our part in the story of His glory.

OVERVIEW
Steve Hoke and Bill Taylor

This hands-on workbook has been designed for two kinds of people: those who have a deep desire to serve God overseas and those who want to help them. It has not been designed to persuade people to become missionaries. Rather, it assumes an initial interest—an early indication or drive somewhere inside that God may have more for you than you previously thought. It assumes an initial commitment to pursue the options. It is aimed at two primary readers: college/university students and young career persons, as well as committed older adults facing the challenge of an early retirement or career change. The information this workbook presents will also help churches, campus groups, schools, missionary training centers, and agencies to think and pray through short-term and long-term plans with those responding to God's call.

Let's Clarify a Couple of Key Items

Are we writing this workbook for the short-term missionary or the longer-term one? The answer in a sense is both, although we are profoundly convinced of the need for longer-term cross-cultural servants of all varieties who will invest a decade or more of their lives in order to pack heaven with worshipers from all peoples, languages, tribes, and nations. This will happen in part through the work of short-term workers—their service and later intercession and mobilizing. But heaven will fill with these peoples primarily because men and women left their homes and cultures to cross language, cultural, and geographic barriers in order to

share Christ and see His church come to maturity. So we have to be up front with you. Bill and I are both totally committed to short-termers, but our heart's desire is to see a vast new battalion of young and older adults in long-term cross-cultural work.

Secondly, what or who really is a missionary? Few words within the evangelical missions vocabulary generate more diverse definitions than "missionary." For some, "everybody is a missionary," but then, if everybody is a missionary, then nobody is a missionary. A few argue that only a select and highly spiritual category of persons is honored with this title; still others discard the title totally and substitute "apostolic messenger" instead. What can we then suggest? By the way, the broader term, "mission," speaks of the most encompassing and holistic task that God has given His church to fulfill in the world.

> *The New Testament affirms that the apostolic messenger (the missionary) becomes the person authoritatively sent out by God and the church on a special mission with a special message, with particular focus on the gentiles/nations.*

In the New Testament, the Greek term *apostello* emerges in two major categories: as a broadly used verb, meaning to send in one form or another and by different senders (132 times), and as a more specifically used noun, the apostolic person (80 times). The core New Testament meaning clusters around ideas related to sending and/or crossing lines, to those being sent, the sent ones—whether messengers or the Twelve, or the others who serve with some kind of apostolic authority or function. The New Testament affirms that the apostolic messenger (the missionary) becomes the person authoritatively sent out by God and the church on a special mission with a special message, with particular focus on the gentiles/ nations.

Other Jewish records show the use of this term describing authorized messengers sent into the Diaspora for special assignments. The New Testament adopts some of these ideas, as well as a broader one from Greek culture that gives the concept of divine authorization. It then injects new meaning into the missionary apostles (lifelong service, Spirit-empowered, with particular focus on the missionary task), referring to the original Twelve (plus Paul) as well as other authorized messengers.

Ironically, as the Latin language takes over Bible use and church life, the synonym, *mitto*, becomes the dominant word, and from this we create the English word "missionary." Therefore, an "accident" of linguistic history has replaced the original Greek concept with all of its richness and depth. In the immediate post-apostolic era, the term was used of itinerant ministers. Roman Catholic usage emerges by 596 A.D. when Gregory the Great sends the Benedictine monk Augustine to lead a missionary delegation to the British Isles. The Roman Church will also use the term "sent ones" in reference to their monastic orders.

The Protestant Reformation, partially in reaction to the Roman positions, minimized the term and concept of the missionary. It re-emerged with greater significance with the Moravians, who used the term for their broad-spectrum enterprise, and then it was adopted by the pioneers, Carey, Judson, Morrison, Livingstone, and their successors in the late 1790s and into the 1800s.

We are convinced that "missionary" is simply not a generic term for all Christians doing everything the church does in service to the kingdom of God. We do a disservice to the "missionary" by universalizing its use. While all believers are witnesses and kingdom servants, not all are missionaries. We do not glamorize nor exalt the missionary, nor ascribe higher honor in life nor greater heavenly reward; neither do we create an artificial office.

This conclusion comes from a biblical theology of vocations (God has given us diverse vocations and all are holy, but not all are the same), a theology of gifts (not all are apostles, nor do all speak in tongues—1 Cor. 12:29; therefore, not all Christians are missionaries), and a theology of callings (the Triune God sovereignly calls some to this position and task). These men and women are cross-cultural workers who serve within or outside their national boundaries, and they will cross some kind of linguistic, cultural, or geographic barriers.

Charting the Course

It isn't easy to become an effective missionary. The road from where you stand, whether in North America, Western Europe, or "Down Under," to the place of effective cross-cultural service is full of roadblocks, detours, and potential false starts. It's easy to get discouraged. That's why we have mapped out 10 steps to help you chart a course from here to the nations.

A lifetime cannot be planned in one sitting with a workbook or with one program on the latest computer. But with some grasp of the available information, you can gain an overview of what lies ahead. You will need to stay close to the Lord and be led by His Spirit as you move toward the nations. This workbook attempts such an overview. It also provides several checklists and worksheets so you can put dates on the benchmarks you pass on the way. It will also periodically ask you to take some time to reflect critically on the journey and to journal—to intentionally reflect, through writing out what God is saying to you, what you are learning and how you are growing.

This handbook describes three phases of missionary development. Each phase includes steps that should be taken as one moves through each phase. Although these steps are ordered sequentially, this is not a mechanical ordering. You will be able to adapt the sequence to your own personal circumstances. There are also

This workbook has been designed for two kinds of people: those who have a deep desire in their hearts to serve God cross-culturally and those who want to help them. It has been designed to help you work through the process of charting a course from where you are to where God would have you be.

It describes the path to cross-cultural service in 10 steps. Each step presents a basic explanation of the importance of that phase of the process, and it provides adequate room for you to keep notes, journal, and gather information you collect. Each step also has a place for you to work, reflect, plan, and pray. There is an extensive resource section in the back of this workbook that provides further information you may need.

Your own journey will be unique. Charting your journey will be a life-changing process. You and the nations await each other.

side roads you may take as you integrate personal information and opportunities with our suggestions.

The format is simple: after the background of each step is discussed, you are asked to respond to a number of questions. These will guide your reflection on what you have been thinking and will help you keep a journal of where you are on this exciting journey.

There's a lot to learn about missions and a cross-cultural career. Each step along the way has its own external sources from which you can draw. Rather than expecting you to wade through every available resource, we've listed some selected ones for you at the end of the workbook.

Let's be honest. Heading into missions can be rather a wild ride. You may see it as a long road, a winding path, a pitching roller coaster, or a cresting wave. But that's what life is, and trying to ride the crest of the wave with Christ is what the Christian life is all about. It won't be easy. All of us have been tested and tempted to drop out. We've all made mistakes. But we didn't bail out, and we're so glad we hung in there during the tough times. We did it for our King and for His kingdom! Christ will walk with you and accompany you to the nations if that's where He wants you. You can trust Him. He was in the boat with the disciples. He's with you even as you read this line.

PREPARATION AND TRAINING PATH: ESSENTIAL STEPS IN THE PROCESS

There are three major phases of missionary preparation and training. Each of these has a number of steps that go together. They can be clustered in the following manner:

Phase 1: Getting Ready – Stretching
- Personal spiritual formation (being)
- Body boost: getting on-the-job experience at home (doing)
- Exposure to other cultures (doing)
- Basic education (knowing)

Phase 2: Getting There – Linking
- Church and agency contact and candidacy
- Ministry assignment search
- Hands-on missionary training

Phase 3: Getting Established – Bonding
- Apprenticeships and internships
- Lifelong learning
- Finishing strong

Phase 1: Getting Ready – Stretching

The introduction will define what a missionary is and will give you a clear profile of the distinct missionary/cross-cultural roles still needed today. It will also provide a yardstick by which to measure and evaluate your present position.

Step 1: Personal spiritual formation. Who you are—your character and spiritual formation as a disciple of Jesus Christ—is essential to the role you will play and to what you do in missions. Clarifying your basic commitment, your "call," and your spiritual gifts and making sure your spiritual foundation is solid are necessary first steps to ensure an effective journey. Finding a personal mentor early on in this journey is foundational to starting well.

Step 2: Body boost: Getting on-the-job experience at home. Understanding your church's unique missions vision and finding your place and gifted role in it are critical to your ultimate effectiveness in extending the church into other cultures. Making disciples in your home culture will hone your ministry skills and help sharpen your spiritual giftedness before serving in a cross-cultural setting. Investing financially in missions will accelerate your own education and establish a lifelong habit.

Step 3: Exposure to other cultures. Growing up in only one culture limits our ability to understand others, appreciate diversity, and learn other languages. Frankly, being monocultural is really boring for today's global citizen in a pluralistic society. So gain some early cross-cultural exposure. It will stretch your mental, physical, and spiritual muscles and will help you understand and accept people of other cultures. It's also an invaluable crucible for testing your gifts, your passions, your dreams, and your capacity for a longer-term commitment.

Step 4: Basic education. Academic preparation for a short- or long-term ministry needs to be customized to your experience, skills, and gifts. What kind of formal training and education do you need for missions today, whether at the level of vocational or professional equipping? What steps can you take at this point that will broaden your worldview and enrich your basic educational background?

Phase 2: Getting There – Linking

Step 5: Church and agency contact and candidacy. What sending group or "team" (church or agency) is the best fit for you as the vehicle for service? Your best work is not a solo effort. What kind of team do you need to make you most effective and to help you grow the most? What kind of team leader do you need to stay focused and effective? What are the options? How do you think through the various possibilities?

Step 6: Ministry assignment search. Related to the question of the mission sending group are the questions of location, people group, and specific role on a church planting team that God is asking you to fulfill in reaching others with the gospel. Who are they? Where are they? How can your gifts be used in reaching those people or in building up the national church? What is your lifelong assignment in God's overall game plan?

Step 7: Hands-on missionary training. Language and culture learning are part of a missionary's "Basic Training" in the hands-on and practical side of living among and relating to people who need the Lord. What are the various ways to gain the most practical skill training outside the classroom?

Phase 3:
Getting Established – Bonding

Step 8: Apprenticeships and internships. Effective missionaries don't just emerge fully formed from their educational experience. On-the-job ministry either at home or on the field tests what you've learned, provides models in ministry, and helps you develop your own approaches for "telling the story" and establishing vital faith for communities (churches). Mentoring in initial ministry ensures a healthy start.

Step 9: Lifelong learning. When missionaries stop learning, they can wither or get stuck. We want to stay alive and growing during this season of our life. Establishing a lifelong learning pattern early in your career is essential to finishing well over the long haul.

Step 10: Finishing strong. Understanding what it means to finish well is crucial, particularly in an activistic Christian subculture that values high accomplishment and activity. Why do so many leaders tend not to finish well, and how can we anticipate these pitfalls? We want to help you intentionalize your spiritual development so that you can grow stronger from cross-cultural service rather than weaker, and all during your Christian pilgrimage you will walk the long path of obedience in the same direction—whether you are in missions or not.

> *Charting your journey is not so much about planning a vacation as it is about becoming intentional in joining God's foreign policy.*

Charting your journey is not so much about planning a vacation as it is about becoming intentional in joining God's foreign policy. It's taking time to pray and plan how you are going to get actively involved. It's about taking specific steps forward rather than being shoved around sideways by peer and career pressure. It's about moving from the grandstand to the playing field, whether as a grower or a goer. Your own journey will be unique. And charting your journey will be a life-changing process. These 10 steps will help you transform your ideas and commitment into a powerful plan for spiritual change.

THE MISSIONARY NEEDED TODAY:
PROFILE OF A CRITICAL ROLE

Steve Hoke

Before you get started on your journey, it may be helpful to take a look at the kind of missionary who's needed today. In the past, many missionaries were often sent out by agencies after training at colleges or seminaries. Knowledge was emphasized—the accumulation of facts and methods a student was expected to need in missionary ministry. It was assumed that once on the field, a graduate would be able to draw on this reserve of information.

The trouble with this approach is that much more is required of a missionary than knowing the right stuff. Cross-cultural service is a crucible that tests one's character and stretches one's ministry skills, while still demanding a wide range of background knowledge. The best way to develop a sound missionary training curriculum is to determine the desired outcomes—what a missionary needs to *be,* and be able to *know* and *do,* and then build backwards to develop all the resources needed to reach those goals. This description of qualities and competencies creates a verbal picture—a profile—which defines outcome goals in a holistic manner, specifically focusing on the character qualities, ministry skills, and knowledge goals needed for effectiveness in ministry. It is an important shift from concern only with what individuals need to *know*, to who they *are* and what they can *do* as a result of training.

In the past several years, a fresh consensus has emerged among "stakeholders" in the missionary training task. Effective missionaries have been recognized as the people best able to identify the qualifications necessary for missionary service. So quality and competency profiles have been designed based on the input from these missionaries. A forum of missionaries, trainers, mission agency leaders, sending pastors, and leaders of receiving churches has prayerfully described what a missionary profile should look like. This consensus approach is critical in creating commitment to change in training programs. The single profile generalizes (for the sake of space) the most critical elements for parallel roles, including the cross-cultural mentor/ coach and tentmaker.

Pages 26-27 contain an abbreviated profile of one distinctive role for North Americans to fill in the global missionary enterprise.* This is only one of a variety of important missionary roles needed today, including the tentmaker, the mentor/coach, the Bible translator, and the provider of technical services. Yes, the new North American cross-cultural servant-leaders of the future will carry out differing roles. Some of the new emerging force will be facilitators, along-side trainers; others will be leadership developers; yet others will be specialists. Most will work side by side with colleagues from other nations. Some will work under non-Western leadership.

But we have chosen this as a baseline profile which can be adapted to other roles. Also, many of you will serve on teams, and this is good news. That means you don't have to have in maximum totality all the qualities desired in the church planting profile. But you must major on the character issues, as well as those critical skills and knowledge components that you don't want

---

* See Robert W. Ferris (Ed.). *Establishing Ministry Training.* Pasadena, CA: William Carey Library, 1995.

to serve without. So as we evaluate these profiles, remember what role we are profiling in each one.

Personalize the Profile

Spend time reading through the basic profile. It is designed as a self-assessment tool. As you read across each row from left to right, check off the competencies you think you have developed, and record your total score in the far right column. For example, for "Spiritual Maturity" you may have checked off four of the six for a score of 4.

Do this for the entire chart; then total your scores in the last box. That numeric score is an objective indication of your level of competency for that role at the present time—before any further training.

You can reassess yourself periodically during your preparation to evaluate what progress you are making in each of the categories. Each time you reassess your progress, note your total score and the stage in your preparation.

HOW TO USE THE PROFILE
Bill Taylor

Welcome to our profile! We offer one profile which combines the most critical character qualities, ministry skills, and knowledge goals for your evaluation. Obviously, one profile cannot identify all the necessary competencies for every possible missionary role—especially those skills needed by specialists in areas such as translation, medicine, technology, the arts, or community development. But it does identify the core competencies needed by most missionaries in the decade ahead. We see at least six different groups of people who will profit from these profiles.

1. Missionary candidates. A young couple named Raquel and David saw an initial draft of the profile. With enthusiasm, David began reading the material, exclaiming, "This is what I need right now! It will enable me to evaluate who and what I should be in terms of character, skills, and knowledge, and our pastor will be encouraged to see the important role our church has in shaping us for cross-cultural ministry."

Missionary candidates have the primary responsibility for their own development and ministry effectiveness. This profile becomes a very helpful tool for them to use as they evaluate the process of preparation for cross-cultural ministry. Potential tentmaker missionaries will also find the profile helpful to identify the general competencies needed, though not specifically applied to that unique role. They will want to be careful to build on the character qualities basic to church planting missionaries.

The mentor/trainer is a more focused role for the more mature missionary who has been seasoned by experience or the new missionary with extensive experience in church planting or renewal work. The key is for the person to have a heart for equipping and proven coaching and mentoring skills. This person also has to be able to work well under and alongside national authority.

2. Local sending churches. A radically new attitude is transforming churches as they recognize and reaffirm their primary role in the selecting, screening, training, and equipping of missionary candidates. At the same time, churches realize there are some tasks they should not tackle alone and others which can be delegated. Among these are specialized training (linguistics, TESOL, technology courses) and deeper biblical/theological/missiological study (whether Islamics, cross-cultural church planting, or knowledge-focused courses). Instead of sending missionaries unprepared, the wise church will utilize all available resources to prepare its missionaries.

3. Missions mobilizers. The key men and women, gifted with ability to encourage, envision, stimulate, and motivate, now have an additional tool which will help them balance enthusiasm with a serious evaluation of the kind of missionary we need.

4. Missionary training schools and programs. The profile suggests to faculty more precisely the kind of learning experiences (formal, non-formal, and/or informal) that will enable the school to produce that kind of missionary. The profile can also help professors identify the teaching/learning objectives they should focus on in their knowledge-oriented courses. For example, professors should teach the missionary basis of the Bible with the explicit objectives of developing a heart for the lost and commitment to world evangelization, as well as enabling their students to engage in missions as a way of life. At the same time, schools and training programs must realize they are partners with the candidates and their churches.

5. Mission agencies or sending organizations. Regardless of the kind of sending group, it's important that the group think critically through exactly what *kind* of missionary it wants to send. It is incumbent on non-church agencies to work in warm dialogue and interdependence with their missionaries' sending churches. Careful use of the profile, with its specific adaptations, will help all sending bodies. Each group will need to modify the profile to fit its specific parameters and requirements.

6. Field based receiving churches. Where there is a receiving church, its leaders have a role in the entire process of equipping the missionary. Obviously, this won't apply to countries where there is no existing church. Overall, the greatest benefit in the profile comes when the six groups enter into mutual dialogue and interdependence in understanding their role in equipping missionaries.

Training Profile of a Cross-Cultural Church Planter: Self-Assessment Tool

Instructions: This profile is designed to assess your own readiness and suitability to serve as a cross-cultural church planter. It is divided into three sections: character qualities, ministry skills, and knowledge goals. Each row lists subcompetencies or qualities for each category, listed in the left column. Entry-level qualities begin in column 1 on the left, progressing toward more advanced ones in the numbered columns to the right. Score one point for each box which describes an area in which you now feel competent. Leave it blank if it is still an area for substantial growth. Tally your scores for each row in the total column on the far right. Sum your row totals on the line at the bottom right. This is an arbitrary number which indicates areas of present strength as well as areas for personal growth.

Once you've completed the profile, take a few minutes to look back over each category to see what that tells you about your level of spiritual experience, maturity, and ministry skill. Consider the following questions:

1. What are the several areas in which I am strong? Is there a pattern that links my church experience with my area of ministry skill? What areas of strength can I continue to build on?

2. What are the areas in which I am weak? Which ones do I want to work on first? How can I begin to make progress on them now?

CROSS-CULTURAL CHURCH PLANTER PROFILE

TRAINING AREA	1	2	3	4	5	6	Total
Character Qualities: The missionary...							
Spiritual Maturity	Knows and loves God; exhibits fruit of the Spirit	Spontaneously worships God; growing in personal and corporate worship	Is responsive to God's guidance; exhibits endurance	Recognizes God's Lordship and leadership; evidences obedience and submission	Is committed to world evangelization; has a clear vocational calling	Is growing in use of spiritual gifts and disciplines, especially prayer and time in the Word	
Family Wholeness (for couples)	Both spouses practice mutual submission and loving service	Freely expresses feelings and empathizes with others	Nurtures and trains children lovingly	Protects planned time and recreation for family	Encourages each family member in spiritual and ministry growth	Relates to the larger mission family/ community	
Single Wholeness (for singles)	Accepts single status, yet open to change	Expresses feelings and empathizes with others; no un-resolved conflict among friends	Able to give and receive in nurturing relationships	Protects planned time and recreation	Aware of parti-cular challenges of being single in a cross-cultural context	Healthy relation-ships with singles and married, whether expatriates or nationals	
Servant's Heart	Accepts God's love and forgive-ness; growing in grace	Submits to Christ's Lordship in trust and obedience	Puts others above self; actively serves to meet needs of others	Serves others with diligence, faithfulness, and joy	Gravitates to the needy	Models the example of Christ	
Adaptability	Recognizes God's sovereignty	Gladly accepts difficult circumstances	Adapts flexibly to new situations; is resilient	Appreciates various person-alities and styles of leadership	Evidences contentment in various settings	Distinguishes between what's "wrong" and what's "different"	
Cultural Sensitivity	Appreciates and values the host culture	Sensitive to host culture's expectations and mores	Sensitive to host culture's models of learning and leading	Recognizes the importance of language learning as ministry	Takes responsibility for lifelong language learning	Appreciates appropriate technologies	
Church and Stewardship	Models active participation in a local church at home and in host culture	Reflects Christ's love for the church; gives faithfully	Partners with the national church and supports a missionary	Stewards relationships and activities for maximum long-term impact on planting reproducing churches; challenges and disciples others in giving to missions		Values the heritage of a people and church; learns from their past	
Ministry Skills: The missionary...							
Language Learning	Recognizes the importance of language learning	Listens actively and discerns language sounds and patterns	Disciplines self to practice regu-larly; develops "bonding" relationships	Takes respon-sibility for life-long language learning	Accepts small failures; learns to laugh at mistakes	Uses language in living, learning, and ministry	
Cultural Adaptation/ Contextual-ization	Appreciates and values aspects of the host culture	Copes with cultural differ-ences; lives incarnationally	Exegetes cities, cultures, and communities	Conversant with needs and concerns of target group	Collects relevant data; analyzes and interprets findings accurately	Adapts behavior and contextualizes appropriately	

Evangelism and Discipleship	Shares Christ in culturally appropriate ways	Leads people to Christ and enfolds in local church	Disciples new believers in Word, prayer, witness, and fellowship	Equips believers to reproduce and have a heart for lost in local communities	Motivates others to use spiritual gifts; engages in spiritual warfare	Empowers and releases disciples to personal ministry	
Church Planting and Development	Prays strategically	Analyzes the social environment	Builds relationships; can grow cell groups of new believers	Develops an effective evangelistic strategy	Trains small group leaders to train others; multiplies cells	Establishes a reproducing congregation(s)	
Leadership Development	Identifies, nurtures, and equips potential leaders	Helps believers interpret and apply the Word in their context	Equips believers in appropriate Bible study methods	Empowers and entrusts others for responsibility	Plans/equips for transitions in partnership with national leaders	Plants churches which contextualize biblical leadership styles	
Leadership/ Followership Skills	Envisions new ministries; enlists others in vision	Uses historical insights to teach churches	Motivates, recognizes, and celebrates others' contributions	Matches appropriate biblical leadership style with situation	Functions as team player and servant-leader	Ministers in Word, deed, and power of the Triune God	
Interpersonal Relationships	Affirms others; not monopolizing or domineering	Willing to listen, especially when corrected	Builds accountable relationships; respectful of spiritual authority	Properly relates to locals and coworkers of opposite gender; not overly intimate	Experienced in community living; can manage conflict without explosion	Relates well to people of different personalities and cultural backgrounds	
Professional Bivocational Skills (Tentmaker)	Strong biblical theology of vocation and ethics	Adequate professional qualifications to match openings in host country	Integrates occupation with ministry; has mindset of application to host culture	Manages self effectively; organizes work efficiently	Maintains personal and organizational accountability	Successfully engages in multiple, simultaneous tasks	

Knowledge Goals: The missionary should comprehend...

Foundational Bible Truths	Biblical story and missionary nature of the Bible	Biblical holism; life and ministry of Jesus	Bible study and interpretation principles and methods	God, Christ, Holy Spirit; spiritual gifts; human nature and destiny	Salvation, including sanctification, victory in Christ, ethics, etc.	Principles of Christian living; the church; apologetics	
Ministry and Missions	Church/ mission partnership theory and strategies	Evangelistic methods and strategies	Developmental principles of spiritual growth and formation	Church planting and growth theory and strategies	Religious history of target people; missions history	Christian spiritual classics; religious dynamics; pluralism	
Leadership and Servanthood	Biblical bases and values; theory of leadership emergence	Principles of spiritual growth and empowerment	Mentoring processes; motivational strategies	Team-building and coordination strategies	Management principles: time/event/ relationships	Servanthood and followership	

TOTAL: ____

EVALUATING YOUR READINESS: FROM A REAL CASE STUDY

Bill Taylor

Mark and Mary, Karl and Susan are my friends. They are two married couples—four young adults. Four cross-cultural servants in difficult contexts within the 10/40 Window. How did they get there?

Ultimately, it was the sovereign seeking and sending God who thrust them into their high-risk, long-term ministries. But this Savior also used university campus ministries to challenge and disciple them, formal and non-formal college studies, graduate school and seminary. In the process, each of these Christians came to that profound conviction—some call this "the call"—that the Lord of the universe wanted them in missions. Mark became an engineer, Mary a teacher, Karl an archaeologist, and Susan a medical technologist. Mark spent a few years in student ministry to gain maturity and experience. Mary discipled younger women. Karl studied three years in seminary while his wife worked, and then he worked in order for Susan to have an intensive year of biblical preparation prior to cross-cultural service. The two couples have had significant

experience in local church ministry, then were sent by these committed and loving churches, and have been sustained by God through tough times.

Mark and Mary have completed two intensive years of nonstop language study in Asia, have welcomed their second child, and have made a major move with their larger team to their target people group. Karl and Susan have more years under their belt—and more ministry scars and sicknesses, to boot! Following language study, they began the long process of building trust relationships, and building their family. Their three children were all born in their country of service.

My four friends have been well trained, at least as much as is possible when you don't know the future. I believe they were effectively equipped. Were they efficiently equipped? That's harder to say; "efficient" is difficult to measure.

Mark and Mary will directly apply their training and disciplines to bivocational ministry. Karl has found that his archaeological skills serve as a means to gain credibility and permission to travel. Amazing doors have opened to him, but he has realized that a full-time archaeology career is not easy. Susan's professional skills, for now, are being applied to the task of raising a growing family.

Q 1. In what way is your own story similar to or different from the account of these two couples?

_____

_____

_____

Q 2. What do you pick up from them about their long-term commitment to cross-cultural ministry?

_____

_____

_____

Q 3. What insights for *your* training and preparation emerge from their journey?

_____

_____

_____

Equipping for the Long Haul: Guiding Principles for Adequate Pre-Field Missionary Training

1. Seek equipping/training specifically applicable to your ministry goals. Choose your missionary ministry: evangelist, church planter, relief and development worker, leader developer, youth worker, tentmaker, teacher, coach/mentor, writer, nurse, doctor, medical technician, graphic artist, computer wizard, radio/television producer—whatever. No matter what you desire to do, you'll need training in order to serve with long-term effectiveness and fruitfulness.

Karl and Susan's target population and ministry goals called for them to seek further training beyond the university that would equip them well for cross-cultural service. For this reason, they sought a graduate school/seminary with a strong missions curriculum. I remember the long hours Susan worked in the hospital to put bread on the table and pay Karl's school bills. Later I admired Karl's commitment to paint houses and hang wallpaper for a year in order for his wife to reach her dream of intensive biblical study. Together they would serve in the Muslim world, and they wanted extensive knowledge of Scripture, theology, and missions before embarking on their career overseas. I won't forget Karl's statement to me, "It will take me 10 years to get proficient in Arabic, and I want to know the Koran thoroughly in order to effectively communicate the story of Christ."

If you want to be a church planter, seek a team with a strong combination of gifts and training. All team members should have strong church experience in their home culture, including a supervised internship. Some team members would benefit from one to four years of solid biblical/theological/missiological study.

They will never regret the years spent in preparation, particularly when they see that study applied in a variety of ways on the field.

Q 1. Into what kind of ministry do you feel God may be leading you? Why? _____

_____

_____

Q 2. How did you come to these conclusions? What confirmations have you seen already? _____

_____

_____

_____

2. Seek equipping/training that will shape you in three major areas: character, skills, and knowledge. These three components woven together will equip you for significant ministry.

Many people think that a Bible college or seminary will do the complete job of preparing them for missions service. It won't. Most formal schools tend to focus on knowledge first and secondly on skills for ministry. Very few have distinguished themselves for their commitment to character development, spirituality, and relationality.

You do need a strong component of knowledge for effective ministry. But it should be knowledge that is directed to produce godliness, character formation, spirituality, and ministry skills. Ask your pastor or spiritual mentor how best to prepare for missions. In addition to the profiles on the previous pages, here are some "competency categories" to keep in mind:

Character: Personal walk with God, spiritual discipline, self-discipline, personal and spiritual maturity, moral purity, personal and family wholeness, a servant's attitude, teachability, adaptability, compassion, spiritual gifting.

Ministry/competency: Relational abilities, evangelism and discipleship gifts, church planting and development skills, language and culture training, communication aptitudes, leadership/followership ability, practical talents, professional/vocational expertise.

Knowledge: Biblical and theological truth, culture basics, communication and language-learning principles, ministry and missions foundations, leadership/followership development, an understanding of global partnership, a basic grasp of human personality and health issues, professional/occupational training, and bivocational issues.

Q 1. In which of the *character* traits above would you say you are relatively strong today? _____

_____

_____

In which do you need strengthening? _____

_____

Q 2. In which *ministry* skills are you strong today? _____

_____

Which skills need strengthening? _____

_____

Q 3. In which *knowledge* areas do you feel you are rather strong? _____

_____

What knowledge areas need strengthening? _____

_____

Mark and Mary's target population required them to enter the country as professionals working with a corporation. Their academic preparation as an engineer and a teacher opened doors, facilitated visas, and legitimized their "work" through a high theology of vocation. Their years of practical ministry had honed their spiritual skills and endurance. And their years of preparation equipped them for the discipline of two years' study in their adopted nation.

3. Seek equipping/training in non-formal, formal, and informal contexts. All three of these aspects of learning are very important, though we tend to think that training must come in formal school contexts.

Non-formal education refers to out-of-the-classroom learning, yet it is designed and purposeful. It includes supervised field trips, internships, and discipling/mentoring relationships. Some non-formal equipping is taught; some is simply "caught."

Informal education refers to the dynamics of living, observing, and learning within community. Much of this is "caught."

Formal education is what we know best. It's what we call "school"—planned, supervised, academic, primarily theoretical, classroom oriented, graded by examinations and graduations and degrees. Certain components of knowledge are best and most efficiently communicated in formal settings.

Where can you get the necessary educational balance? First, use the worksheet below to think through your own best learning and experiences and identify in which category (non-formal, informal, formal) they fall. Notice that some learning experiences overlap into two or even three contexts.

Now think in terms of seven different learning contexts that mold a future missionary:

1. The **home** shapes us.

2. The **job/marketplace** teaches and hones skills.

3. The **church** stimulates development of character, ministry skills, and a degree of important knowledge.

4. **Formal schools** focus on knowledge and some skills.

5. **Mission agencies** take a careful look at character, skills, and knowledge and may offer their own specific equipping.

6. The **future national church** you may serve with will shape you in all areas of your life.

7. Other kinds of **interpersonal relationships** mold us.

Now go back to the character, skill, and knowledge dimensions. Where are these best learned in relation to the seven learning contexts? This exercise can help you determine the best route to follow in your own equipping/training process as you contemplate missions.

Q 1. In which *informal* contexts have you learned important lessons? _____

_____

What lessons did you learn? _____

_____

_____

Q 2. Which *non-formal* contexts have provided significant learning for you? _____

_____

In what areas? _____

_____

Q 3. List the different schools you've studied in, and total the years. That's the part of your life that you've spent "institutionalized." _____

_____

In what ways has this been good and/or not so good for you? _____

_____

_____

_____

Q 4. What other kinds of *formal* learning contexts could be valuable to you as you prepare for cross-cultural service? _____

_____

_____

_____

Finally...

"Just a minute!" you might interject. "This seems to be only for the long-term missionary! What about those of us who are committed to short-term missions? We're open to long-term, but we want to start short-term!"

Well, it depends on **how long** your short term is, **where** you go, **what you do** when you get there, **whom you go with**, and **how old** and **how mature you are**.

If you're going for a prayer journey into the 10/40 Window, you definitely need preparation in certain character, skills, and knowledge. Make a list of which competencies you need in these three areas.

If you're going to do mime and street evangelism for a summer, you also need specific preparation/training in character, skills, and knowledge. List here which competencies you need in these three areas.

If you're going to teach English in Hungary or China for a year or two, if you are going to help construct a church or school building or service computers, again you'll need specific preparation/training in character, skills, and knowledge. Make a list of the competencies you need, and take the initiative for developing in each area you identify.

Q   1. What kind of short-term ministry do you see yourself moving into in the near future?

_____

_____

_____

Q   2. What specific kinds of equipping will you need in the following areas?

     a. Character/spirituality _____

_____

     b. Ministry skills _____

_____

     c. Knowledge _____

_____

Q   3. Where do you think you can acquire the preparation you need? _____

_____

_____

Why Am I Telling You All This?

What I'm trying to establish is that we need effective (and efficient) equipping/training for all types of cross-cultural ministry. And the longer the ministry time commitment, the more serious the equipping/training must be. Don't try to cut it short!

> Heaven will be full of worshipers of the Lamb who are there because someone left home for years and crossed geographical, language, and cultural barriers.

I'm not saying you have to get a master's or doctorate in missions before you can serve cross-culturally. But I know of very few experienced missionaries who regret their training, even if it meant years of study, discipline, and waiting. It taught them perseverance and spiritual maturity, equipping them for effective, hang-in-there, cross-cultural ministry.

(Be aware, however, of the danger inherent in getting further training too soon. I have friends who became sidetracked and lost their passion for the world. Some bought into the "American dream" so much that they gave up their original vision.)

Years of training have equipped the long-term missionaries I know for long-term, cross-cultural ministry. And they were there long enough to enjoy the fruit of their work. Of course it was tough. Yes, they got sick. What did they expect? But they saw God at work, and heaven will be full of worshipers of the Lamb who are there because someone left home for years and crossed geographical, language, and cultural barriers to present the powerful, supernatural, living Jesus Christ to people who had not known Him.

My friends Mark and Mary, Karl and Susan all had significant short-term experiences before heading into long-term service. Their short-term service called for short-term training, and they were thankful for it. Their long-term training took more time. But if you ask them whether it was worth it, they respond with a resounding, "YES!"

Phase 1:
Getting Ready – Stretching

Step 1: Personal Spiritual Formation

Step 2: Body Boost: Getting on-the-Job Experience at Home

Step 3: Exposure to Other Cultures

Step 4: Basic Education

STEP 1: PERSONAL SPIRITUAL FORMATION

Steve Hoke

You're a growing Christian. You know Jesus Christ as your Savior and are getting to know Him as Lord of your life and Hope of the world. You're His disciple, and you want to grow as a globalized Christian—a believer with a heart for the world and a passion to take the gospel to all peoples.

You've made a commitment. You love God and want to serve Him. You believe He may be leading you to take on one of the most rewarding roles in the world—to become a cross-cultural messenger/missionary.

Dedication is not enough. Raw zeal is not enough. Commitment is not enough. Not even "high octane" spiritual gifts are enough! We need to be constantly growing in an intimate relationship with Christ.

Paul told the Philippians they needed to look forward, not back. He chided them to forget the past and to press toward the goal of knowing Christ more intimately. Growth in Christ takes place as you nurture your faith relationship through prayer, the study of God's living Word, spiritual disciplines, Christian witness, and fellowship with other Christians in the church community.

Relationship is everything. This is true from the Trinity on through to Christ and His disciples, to the church today. Who you are is more important than what you do. For that reason alone, it's critical to get your relational priorities straight from the outset. As you prepare yourself in right relationship with the Lord of the universe, you'll find that your ministry will flow out of your being—your internal spiritual character and your intimacy with Christ.

The "Perspectives on the World Christian Movement" course being taught in many churches in the world helps students see that the Bible is "The Story of His Glory." From Genesis through Revelation, the Bible is the story of God drawing a people to Himself—into a relationship of love, acceptance, and forgiveness. Eugene Peterson has expressed the worship dimension in even more obvious terms: "God is personal reality to be enjoyed.... We are re-deemed so that we are capable of enjoying Him. His grace evokes our gratitude."

Missions, then, is "His-story"—God's process of calling disciples from every nation to follow Him and give Him glory as "true worshipers." So as we go and make disciples, our essential task is to call the peoples and nations of the world to worship Him too. And when Christ finally returns, all of us who follow Him will get to take part in the massive international worship service that's previewed in Revelation 5–7 and that is going on right now!

Are you learning to pray? The Bible tells us that the way to *be* anything, to *get* anywhere, and to *do* anything is to pray. Pray-ers become doers. The same disciples whom Jesus commanded to pray for workers for the harvest (Matt. 9:37-38) were the ones He sent to reap the harvest (Matt. 10:1-23).

Every surge of missionary activity in history has grown out of revitalized personal prayer and personal renewal. If you're serious about being sent, your concern for those who need to be reached will drive you to pray for them and for the missionaries who are trying to reach them. Pray alone. Pray with others. Get involved in some of the prayer events in the worldwide prayer movement for world evangelization, such as concerts of prayer or prayer summits.

> *Every surge of missionary activity in history has grown out of revitalized personal prayer and personal renewal.*

Prayer is fed by passion and reality. Fuel your prayer with well-focused information. Constantly try to discover and define the needs of this world God loves. Use material like *Operation World* or a daily prayer journal to pray for peoples and nations.

One of the best ways to give meaning to facts is to relate them to individuals you know. So take part in supporting an expatriate or national missionary. Get to know them: read their prayer letters and correspond with them. Talk to them by e-mail or when they're on home leave. Pray for their work.

Are you learning to give? Have you started supporting someone in missions? Are you supporting someone "behind the scenes" as well as on the "front lines"? Have you considered living more simply now so that you can give more to advancing God's kingdom? You don't have to wait until you are on a missionary income to live within a missionary budget. A "faith" missionary becomes a steward of the gifts of others. You give up the luxury of generating a predictable income in exchange for vocational involvement in God's worldwide purpose. The missionary embraces a "wartime" living allowance according to need as an expression of wise stewardship.

Are you studying God's Word? Do you have a consistent approach to exposing yourself not only to what the Bible says but what it calls you to do? Are you in a study group with others who are attempting to understand God's will for them through studying His Word? Are you adjusting your life to what it demands of you? Do you hold each other responsible for obedience? Are you memorizing portions of God's love letter to you? Are you growing in your foundational understanding?

What is your sense of God's "call" on your life? This is a commonly used and often misunderstood term. The Spirit uses various routes to thrust us into missions. Whether our heart's desires lie in bivocational tentmaking or in long-term vocational missions, we relate to a God who loves us and knows us intimately, and who wants to work with us according to our uniqueness.

The letter on pages 36-37 is our actual response to a young couple seeking clarity on what this "call" might be and how to deal with it.

Are you involved with other Christians? 1 Corinthians 12 tells us that when we become Christians, we not only join God's family as adopted sons or daughters, but we also become part of a marvelous organism called the Body of Christ. Each of us has been gifted to build up the others. Christians simply cannot live without other Christians.

How are you experiencing Christian fellowship? Are you seriously plugged into a local congregation where you're growing in your commitment to the Body of Christ? Are you involved in a cell based group? Are you serving with your gift (see the profile dimension on local church participation)?

Are you telling the story of the reality of Christ in your own life? The most effective way the gospel can be communicated is through telling others what Christ has done for you. It's essentially storytelling. To want to speak for Christ "out there" without sharing Him with others "here" would be inconsistent, to say the least.

Gifts of story-telling and communicating are developed in practice. Your actions reinforce your values and make them meaningful. You become what you do. Becoming a cross-cultural witness means being a witness right here, right now. The more cross-cultural you can make your witness now, the better equipped you'll be to interact with people of other cultures in the future.

> *Becoming a cross-cultural witness means being a witness right here, right now. The more cross-cultural you can make your witness now, the better equipped you'll be to interact with people of other cultures in the future.*

Is there a fragrance to your life, an unmistakable evidence of the presence of God? The history of Christian mission is strewn with the well-meaning but misdirected lives of people who thought of mission primarily as a task—crusading, preaching, or ministering—and not essentially *relationship*. They got started on the track of *doing* before their life had a quality of *being* that made them attractive. Paul reminds his readers in 2 Corinthians 3:2 that they are "living letters"—people whose lives will be read by those around them. He adds in 1 Corinthians 2:14 that through us Christ spreads the fragrance of His knowledge and love to others.

Is your life becoming increasingly more fragrant and attractive? Does the way you live convey a kind of message the world can find attractive and see? Is God's touch on your life becoming more evident with each year of your Christian experience?

For further insight into the issue of the missionary call, read the following letter that Bill wrote to Kirk and Sarah.

THOUGHTS ON THE MISSIONARY "CALL"

Bill Taylor

Dear Kirk and Sarah,

Your great letter just arrived, and it's good to hear from you again. How we praise God for the deep conviction the two of you have to serve Christ in long-term cross-cultural ministry in Central Europe. You have asked a tough question: "How do we know we are called?" I'm not sure I can fully answer it. You're touching on deep-fiber stuff! It involves critical issues that relate to who we are, how God has made us, our understanding of who God is, and how He directs us today.

Unfortunately, there's a lot of confusing and sometimes contradictory talk going out about the "missionary call." Beware of the extremes! Some require you to have had your own mystical "call" or voice from God. I don't deny this happens, but don't let others over-spiritualize the process, then force it on you as normative. Other Christians approach it from an overly rational, dry, mathematical model that gathers the facts, prays, and then makes a logical decision.

I've concluded that the Spirit uses various routes to thrust us into missions. Whether our hearts' desires are to be inner-city youth ministers, tentmakers in "restricted access" countries, long-term church planters, whatever, we all relate to a God who loves us and knows us intimately, and who wants to work with us according to our uniqueness.

In a sense, we're all "called" of God. Called to Christ, called to worship and serve Him, called to walk worthy of our calling in Him, called to obey the biblical creation mandates, called to share Christ with others.

So, why make a big deal of the "missionary call"? Well, it's partly to clarify matters. We want to eliminate unbiblical teaching that tries to dichotomize vocations and life into secular and sacred. We seek a balance here as we consider the biblical theology of creation and vocation alongside the overarching challenges of using our vocations in cross-cultural service. And this applies to "tentmakers" and "home missionaries" as well as "regular" missionaries!

What Are Some of the Ways That God Leads People Into Missions?

Path 1: A few people really will have some kind of personalized call, vision, powerful encounter, or voice from the Lord. They feel a deep sense of having received a mandate from God. It's incontrovertible. They step out in straightforward obedience to the Spirit. Some of these folks may quote Paul's Macedonian call to back up their experience. But the fact is, Paul was already functioning as a field missionary when this "call" came to him. The Macedonian call served to *reroute* Paul in a different geographic direction than he had been headed. Frankly, I don't use this passage much in terms of the missionary "call." Missionaries who had a strong "personalized call" report that this experience helps sustain them when the going gets really rough. Note that a "personal call" is not a built-in guarantee that one will be a successful missionary.

Path 2: Other friends tell me theirs is not a matter of a "personalized call" to missions. It's more a matter of obedience to God. In some cases the wife saw that her primary call of God was to marry this man, knowing that he was (and therefore, they were) going into missions. God's will thus becomes clear through a combination of circumstances and relationships.

Some have called this the "Ruth/Naomi" model. (You may want to reread that story in the book of Ruth.) This route isn't easy. One missionary wife told me that perhaps had she felt her own kind of calling to missions, it would have made her less susceptible to doubt and questioning during the difficult times on the field. But she hung in there long-term, and I really respect her for it.

Path 3: Still others find that they end up in missions after a serious evaluation of prime factors: deep commitment and obedience to Christ, plus a personal assessment of interests, gifts, experience, and dreams, combined with a heart of compassion for the lost and the poor, and an opportunity to serve and to make a difference in the world. These all converge to form a path into missions. In this example, it's more a case of the best job fit, with conclusions made after much prayer and evaluation.

Path 4: Some report that the prime factors leading them into missions were rather simple: a radical obedience to Christ that meant a willingness to do anything, go anywhere, pay any price, plus an identification of their gifts and others' needs. Discovering this great need provided the final indicator of where and what would constitute a strategic investment of their life and gifts.

Common Factors in the Four Paths

In all four paths, certain common components are crucial. In all there is a passion to serve Christ in a risky venture larger than one's own life. All call for radical obedience to God. All involve an overall process of wise evaluation and of confirmation and guidance from trusted colleagues and spiritual leaders. And in all there is a final, profound, unshaking conviction from the Spirit of God that "this is what God truly has for me." It may be short-term or long-term, far away or just on the other side of town, but "this is what I've got to do with my life."

These are some of my musings after 32 years of being involved in missions. I've seen effective missionaries and poor missionaries from all four "calling" categories. As you have further questions come up, be sure to pop a note off to me. You have my snail-mail and e-mail addresses, so let's keep talking.

In the Lamb,
Bill Taylor

JOURNAL WORKSHEET 1

WHERE ARE YOU NOW?

How would you describe your conversations with God? _____

_____

Are you praying specifically and knowledgeably about your involvement in missions? _____

_____

Are you making a significant financial investment in God's global purposes? _____

_____

How do you keep track of specific requests? Answers? Promises? _____

_____

Describe your Bible reading and study routine. _____

_____

How often are you with other Christians? How are you strengthening one another? _____

_____

How are you growing in your ability to witness to others about your experience with Christ? _____

_____

What are your gifts and aptitudes, and how are you growing in your use of them? _____

_____

_____

How would you describe your "fragrance" and the evidence of God's presence in your life? _____

_____

WHAT DO YOU NEED TO DO NEXT?

I will strengthen my prayer life by... _____

_____

_____

I will increase my financial investment in God's purposes by... _____

_____

_____

I will deepen my understanding and application of God's Word by... _____

_____

_____

I will strengthen my participation in and commitment to Christ's Body by... _____

_____

_____

I will become a more active and effective witness to my faith by... _____

_____

_____

I will learn more about my God-given gifts and aptitudes by... _____

_____

_____

I will practice the presence of God in my life by... _____

_____

_____

WHAT WILL THE FUTURE LOOK LIKE?

What kind of person will you become if you obediently carry out your desire to be more focused in prayer, Bible study, fellowship, witness, and evidencing God's presence in your life?

_____

_____

_____

_____

What marks of true spirituality would you like to see developed in your life over the long term? _____

_____

_____

_____

_____

STEP 2: BODY BOOST: GETTING ON-THE-JOB EXPERIENCE AT HOME

Steve Hoke

Just as you need to grow in your commitment to Christ, you need to grow in your commitment to the Body of Christ. Individual Christians become a part of a larger Christian family when they accept Jesus Christ as Lord. The Bible never describes Christians as being whole unless they're in fellowship with one another. Romans 12 and 1 Corinthians 12 tell us that we are part of one another. We are all parts of the Body of Christ. We're connected and linked together.

You want to be seriously involved in a church—worshiping, fellowshiping, learning, and serving with a local church wherever you are. If you're a college student who became a Christian after you left home for school, this may mean relating to two church bases. You'll need a church-away-from-home as well as participating in your hometown church.

Those preparing for missionary service need to be involved in many ways: they need to be with other Christians on the campus, in the marketplace, on the job, in the training school, and on the field. They need to be in contact with a mission sending body. They need to be serving in a local church.

You may teach a Sunday school class. You could be part of an evangelism team. You could (should) serve in a home/cell church group. You could be a summer intern in church. You need to be a fully functioning Body member who is ministering with his or her spiritual gift.

Ministry is mutual. You must build into the church and make a contribution with your life before you can ever expect to receive from that church. From the local church come not only the people, but also the intercession, counsel, encouragement, and finances that make the worldwide mission enterprise possible.

Share your new commitment with your family and local church. Start with your parents and family and the pastoral team. Share with your shepherds any decisions or commitments you've made about missions. Ask for advice and help. Ask them to give you the spiritual guidance every Christian needs.

Too many young mission zealots neglect their family in the critical early steps of mission enthusiasm. Seek the advice of parents and family members as you begin your exploration. Ask for their specific prayer support. Since they are your most natural supporters, don't neglect nurturing the relationship and communication until you come asking for money. Involve them as active participants early in the process.

Ask: "If you were me, how would you prepare for cross-cultural service?" Let the pastor know that you're genuinely seeking input and that you are available and teachable. You desire to be prepared within the church for effective ministry. Seek wise counsel from other mature Christians in the church as well. In every church are countless creative ways to develop your skills in serving, leading, helping, teaching, witnessing, and discipling. Take part in a number of different tasks within your local congregation that will help you discover your gifts, use them, and sharpen your understanding of what God wants you to do. And remember—you learn to serve by serving. Some of your first roles may best be servant jobs.

> *Ministry is mutual. You must build into the church and make a contribution with your life before you can ever expect to receive from that church.*

Find a fruitful senior saint who can serve as a practical spiritual guide or mentor. Ask leaders in your church and your community if there is a special person or couple who can mentor you and pray with you. This will involve much more than just counseling. Seek a mature person whose kingdom values and lifestyle are evident, and who would be willing to spend regular time with you as a kind of spiritual director. Some churches have a procedure for taking pastoral or missionary candidates "under care" while they're in training for ministry.

Offer to join (or start) the mission committee of your church. Many issues will be clarified in your own mind as you join others in your church as they seek to obey God's foreign policy for the church. Discussion and study of church mission policy and giving will enlarge your own understanding and enlighten your personal giving.

Don't be afraid to ask questions about things that are new to you or that might appear out of sync with what God is teaching you about missions. You may be able to play a helpful role in increasing the energy and effectiveness of your church's involvement in missions.

Increasingly, local churches are assuming greater responsibility in the training of their missionary candidates. This usually involves an intentional "internship" or "apprenticeship" in which specific character qualities and ministry skills are nurtured. The church recognizes such people as having been called to the Christian ministry and seeks to support them through their training period and into their future career. It is also during such a trial period that a church decides whether or not to confirm and stand behind your future ministry.

If your church does not have a strong missions training program, share a copy of this workbook with the leaders. Share what you've learned about yourself through it. Even if your local church is in the dark about the whole process of how to help a person get overseas, you still need their prayers and counsel.

Develop accountable relationships. Two dynamics are critical to your spiritual maturation. First, you need to have strong personal *relationships* in order to have effective ongoing ministry. Our culture's extreme stress on individualism has left Western Christianity weak in relationships. Mentoring relationships for growth should include a relational network that embraces mentors, peers, and younger Christians in order to ensure development and a healthy perspective on life and ministry.

Second, you need mentoring relationships for *accountability*. You should also seek lateral or "peer mentoring" relationships with friends and colleagues with whom you can enter mutually supportive relationships for encouragement and protection. It is precisely the qualities of relaxed, open, and relevant relationships with peers that enable you to stimulate, interact with, and hold one another accountable at a more personal level. A circle of accountability is the safeguard for finishing well. (For more on mentoring, see the "Finding Personal Mentors" exercise on page 110.)

Demonstrate your own commitment in financial stewardship. Show the same kind of commitment you may later want others to show for your ministry. Missions will become more real to you as you invest yourself practically in prayer, financial support, and encouragement for someone in whose shoes you may someday walk. When you are on support yourself, your experience in supporting others will enhance your own ministry to your donors. And the challenge of investing wisely will stimulate you to learn more than you might otherwise.

Much cross-cultural experience can be tapped in the local church. Western Christians travel internationally at an increasing rate. Hook up with some of these travelers and ask them to share their experiences with you. It will help both you and them to deepen your understanding of cross-cultural issues and ministry. Also, talk with missionaries. Invite international students into your home; study with them; hang out with them.

Don't overlook the value of the training you will receive from your job experience. There are important lessons to be learned and values to be developed from any job, no matter how menial.

Missionaries must be people who can become self-sufficient. The next generation of missionaries will have to use their skills to generate income in order to stay on the field. They must be imaginative and find ways to do routine tasks more effectively.

Look at every job as a learning opportunity. Approach it with an open mind and the simple belief that God has placed you in it for a purpose and expects you to do your very best. Learn about taking directions from others. Learn about working on a team. Take initiative. Innovate. Start new ministries.

Develop responsibility in the "earning a living" part of your training. Western young people are not considered "adult" until they have actually gone out and supported themselves. Too often our society, including our schools, treats young adults as if they were not yet ready to accept major responsibility. Don't fall into this trap.

You develop responsibility by proving yourself over time in the various roles you fill. Appreciate what other people say about responsibility and missions. But use every opportunity to sharpen your professional skills while gaining work experience in the marketplace.

As you pray and plan, listen for God's voice and feel God's touch. Try to discover His path for you. As the church helps you, they too will catch a vision. They'll be stretched to seek for more!

You and your church need to plan seriously how the congregation and its leaders will relate to you as a potential missionary. How can they help in your preparation and training? What might be their long-term commitment to you? What is your long-term commitment to them?

For further resources to explore, check out the next two articles.

FOR BEST RESULTS...

Steve Hoke

If you want to best prepare yourself for future ministry, follow this suggested pre-field conditioning program while rooted in your home church and culture.

- **Be accepting of others' opinions.** Acceptance, openness, and trust are three of the most important values you can carry into intercultural relationships. When you talk to people who hold differing viewpoints from yours, ask questions like, "Can you help me understand why...?" instead of trying to convince them that your opinion is better.
- **Refine the art of conversation.** Commit yourself to making new acquaintances. Take the initiative. Ask good questions. Be a responsive listener.
- **Practice adapting/stretching.** Develop flexibility. Consider alternatives. Look for more than one way to accomplish tasks, and practice praising others for their creativity.
- **Be informed about world events.** Become a proactive reader of international news and of materials on intercultural relations. Sharpen your perception of patterns and principles relating Scripture to cultures and peoples' behavior.
- **Study other cultures.** Ted Ward's practical handbook, *Living Overseas*, is an excellent primer. It contains positive tips for learning about other cultures. Study books on cultural anthropology and look for magazine articles describing peoples from other cultures.

- **Get accustomed to another language.** Tune your radio or television to a foreign language station. Learn basic phrases in another language. Practicing any new language sharpens your mental capacities and makes you more responsive to the particular language you will learn overseas.
- **Build a friendship with a person from another country.** Establish a long-range relationship. Learn some of your new friend's language and try to understand his or her perspective.
- **Master the fundamentals of spiritual discipline.** Richard Foster's *Celebration of Discipline* stresses that you must establish inner order before you can expect your outer activity to have coherence and power. Either you enter the arena of spiritual warfare dressed and equipped for battle, or you step out spiritually naked.
- **Strengthen spiritual unity by yielding your rights.** Paul said that all things were permissible, but not all things were beneficial (1 Cor. 10:23). Although some behavior isn't inherently wrong or evil, it doesn't build unity. Paul was willing not to insist on his rights in every situation (Phil. 4:11-12). He accepted certain limitations or conditions (1 Cor. 9:12, 15, 19). Look for ministry opportunities in which you can yield rather than demand your rights.
- **Commit to a team ministry in your church.** Work together with people. Share ideas. Discuss goals. Take leadership responsibility. You must learn to deal graciously with interruptions and ambiguity, give and receive feedback, and have your ideas rejected.
- **Keep a daily journal.** This is a practical way to reflect on your ideas, thoughts, and feelings in a consistent, organized manner. Record what you saw and felt, why you responded the way you did, and what you learned about yourself. Keeping a journal will sharpen your critical thinking and is one way of tracking your spiritual journey.
- **Develop physical stamina.** Physical endurance affects every area of life, especially the spiritual. The physical and emotional demands of entering and adjusting to a new culture can be countered through a consistent conditioning program.
- **Invest financially in advancing God's kingdom**—both on the "front lines" and "behind the scenes." Research where this giving can be most effective; then accompany it with prayer.

Reprinted with permission from *Wherever*, a publication of TEAM.

WHY WAIT TILL YOU GET THERE?

Mala Malmstead

Mission service today offers incredible opportunities to experience the world while sharing Christ. Sometimes our desire for adventure can blind us to the fact that being a missionary for any length of time is hard work. It demands many skills and an uncompromising clarity of purpose.

Just living cross-culturally is often tougher and far more stressful than living at home. Communication barriers, the complications of obtaining basic necessities like food and clean water, and the difficulties of getting along with coworkers and adapting to a new culture may be daily challenges.

On top of all this, your purpose isn't just to survive—it's to point others to Christ. So the more ministry experience you have at home, the more effective you'll be in a foreign context.

Minister at Home

Preparing for your mission experience is the key to adapting well and being a useful instrument, available for what God wants to do through you. If you aren't sure you want to go through the preparation process, maybe you need to reconsider your mission plans. Consider traveling instead—experiencing the world without the express purpose of sharing the gospel.

You can test your missions motivation by examining the activities you're involved in now. The most important way to prepare yourself for the rigors of missions is to live a life of service at home first. Whether you have a year before your proposed mission trip or just a couple of weeks, you can get involved in ministry. Any opportunity that takes you out of your comfort zone is good preparation for the foreign field.

Here are a few ways you can begin to get actively involved in ministry right now, so you'll be better prepared for your future as a missionary.

Find Cross-Cultural Environments

While in college, I was involved in various inner-city outreaches. As I worked at shelters for the homeless, I learned to listen to people from backgrounds and situations vastly different from my own. By volunteering with a kids' mentoring program, I met children from another ethnic group. They spoke an English lingo that I didn't know. Even their jokes and concepts of morality were foreign to me.

Learn to laugh at your mistakes, and don't underestimate the power of gestures and pantomime. The most important thing is not how you communicate—it's that you do communicate.

As a result of these experiences, I was better prepared later to do child evangelism in Spain and to work in orphanages in India and Uzbekistan.

Opportunities for ministry abound! Finding one that suits your personality and interests should not be too difficult. Literacy programs, Sunday schools, church youth groups, crisis pregnancy centers, drama, music, and prison ministries are just a few of the hundreds of options that will help prepare you for overseas ministry.

Practice Telling the Story

Witnessing to friends and strangers in your own country is difficult for most Christians. Knowing your culture and caring what others think can be hard barriers to overcome. But the more you learn to share your faith at home, the more effectively you'll share your faith overseas. It's important to know some basic evangelistic tools and methods, to know how to verbalize your testimony and to be familiar with some Scripture that may speak to non-Christians.

Suzy Schultz is one example of how this works. Before Schultz went to Poland, she spent time witnessing in a local park. She talked with total strangers and shared with them how they could receive Christ.

Later, when two artists she was witnessing to in Poland wanted to receive Christ, Schultz was prepared to explain salvation to them.

Make International Friends

Spending time with international students or with foreigners at your workplace is excellent training for developing friendships abroad.

Scott DeVries spent two years in Czechoslovakia. He says some of his closest friends were international students whom he met while in college and seminary. "They helped me see the world from their eyes," DeVries explains.

Broadening your perspective on the world is crucial to understanding a foreign culture. If you talk to a person from your country of interest, you can learn a great deal about that person's culture long before you enter it.

Knowing as much as you can about the culture you are planning to enter will not only minimize your culture shock, it will also help you avoid some painful blunders. The country you enter may be nothing like your own. You cannot expect it to be.

You can follow these guidelines to prepare for missions right now. You can also take specific steps toward making your transition to the mission field smoother. Below are some suggestions I have found helpful.

Study the Language

I recently returned from a year in Tashkent, Uzbekistan, where two languages are spoken: Russian and Uzbek. I struggled through that year, at times feeling isolated and helpless due to my lack of language training.

Making friends was tough, too. I felt inhibited by the difficulty of communicating. I cannot emphasize strongly enough the importance of spending time learning your target language. While you're still at home, listen to language tapes regularly. Teach yourself from a book or the Internet. Or hire a tutor to help you with the language. Find a national of that country to practice with you and give you pronunciation tips. At the very least, learn a few important phrases as you travel. Not only will you be able to communicate (even if it's only a little bit), but the people you meet will be touched by your efforts with their language.

Study the Country

A very useful book that can give you an overview of the continent and of the specific country you're heading for is *Operation World* by Patrick Johnstone (Zondervan, 1997). Filled with information about the various religions in each region, the state of the church, and the country's key prayer needs, it is an excellent way to learn about "your" country and to begin praying faithfully. Find a world map or atlas so you can visualize the country and familiarize yourself with its geography, cities, and so forth.

While you're at it, get on the Internet. Take a trip to the local library and research the history, traditions, philosophers, famous writers, and scientists of the country. People are extremely proud of their cultural heritage. They may expect you to know their countrymen's accomplishments. Ignorance about their country can strongly offend them.

Involve Your Family and Church

If you're seriously considering a mission trip, you may have approached your family and church already for counsel, service, prayer, and finances. In order for others to be involved in and contributing to your trip, you have to do a lot of networking and sharing your vision. Mission service is not the place for showing off your independence or proving your own capabilities. As David Hicks of Operation Mobilization puts it, "Your mission trip should not only impact you, but should impact lots of people who can't go."

Be a Servant

No matter how much you prepare for cross-cultural work, there will still be things that surprise, challenge, disgust, and disturb you. And though you may try to be the most culturally sensitive person in the world, you probably will end up offending people more than once. These experiences are normal. Maybe the best thing to remember is that the key to effective ministry is servanthood.

One mission leader says that when he looks for mission recruits, he looks for people who are teachable, flexible, and humble in spirit. "Character is more desirable than competence," he says. "If your attitude is [one of] seeking after God, then your life will reflect that in service."

Heading overseas with a warm, caring attitude and finding practical ways to serve the people you want to reach will go a long way toward making your mission experience successful. Cultivate these skills and attitudes now, and you'll be better prepared for cross-cultural service—whenever and wherever God leads you.

Mala Malmstead is a free-lance writer who was raised on the mission field. She and her husband Greg recently spent a year teaching English in Uzbekistan. They currently live in Fairburn, Georgia.

FOUR BUILDING BLOCKS FOR LIFETIME SERVICE

Robertson McQuilkin

God sent His only Son as a missionary to people who were without hope. It was a sacrificial plan, a costly one—but such is His love. The Apostle Paul spoke of himself as a colaborer with God. In God's primary work of redemption, the career missionary is a special apostolic emissary—a credentialed ambassador of the King of all kings!

There are four important building blocks for a life of missionary service. To discover and shape them, you need a team. God has provided this team in His church.

1. Heart Preparation

If your attitudes and behavior don't give people a valid picture of the character of Jesus Christ, what kind of salvation will you have to offer? The key is continual personal sacrifice, ever moving toward a greater likeness to the Savior. The path for this constant personal growth is a solid prayer life—a discipline that is learned over time.

2. Active Involvement in Ministry

Gifts of the Spirit are needed for full-time missionary service. For example, the gift of evangelism is needed for church planting work. There's only one way to know if you have the gifts you need: minister. Try it, find out what your abilities are, and develop them.

But be patient. Give the process time. Don't decide too soon that you don't have a particular gift you think you need. I made this mistake. I assumed that if I had the gift of evangelism I must become a little Billy Graham. I pleaded with God to give me the gift of evangelism and expected people to respond to the gospel in droves when I spoke to a crowd. If I didn't have this kind of gift, how else could I be a pioneer missionary?

Finally, I realized I had restricted my definition of evangelism. I discovered God was preparing me for evangelism in Japan, where mass meetings were not the best way to communicate the gospel. I could settle among unevangelized people and love them to Jesus Christ.

3. Formal Preparation/Basic Education

One of the normal contemporary routes to an effective ministry includes formal study of God, Scripture, and missions. Even those going into support roles in missions, like medicine and technology, can benefit from a year of Bible study. These support people must be able to function as part of the team and participate in winning others to faith and building up the church.

A full degree program in a Bible college or seminary is valuable for those pursuing a career in evangelism or Bible teaching. Find a school that has a strong reputation for preparing full-time missionaries—just as you would choose the best possible medical school if you were preparing to become a doctor. Consult with mission leaders to determine the relative quality of the schools that interest you. (See Step 4, Basic Education, pages 57-61.)

4. Language and Cultural Studies

Don't skimp on these. Don McAlpine arrived in Japan with the conviction that the Communists would take over momentarily or the Lord would return. He never paused long enough to learn the language—or the culture, either.

Using an interpreter for more than 30 years, he became a premier church-starting evangelist. He compensated for his lack of language and his occasional lapses in cultural sensitivity by maintaining a strong prayer life and a deep love for people. Of the hundreds of missionaries I've known, he is the only exception I've found to the rule of careful language and cultural study. (For further information, see Step 7, Hands-On Missionary Training, pages 80-88.)

A Church Home

To fit these four building blocks of a missionary career together properly, build a relationship with at least one church that will give you partnership in vision and prayer. For confirmation of your call, for supervised experience in ministry, for prayer and financial support, for accountability and reinforcement while on the field, there is no substitute for a strong sending church.

When you are ready to choose a mission body and a place of service, one will follow the other. Some feel called to a particular location and look for the mission best suited to reach that particular people. Others choose the agency first, to be sure of the "team" before deciding on the "playing field." If your church sends all its missionaries through a single board, then your choice of a board is predetermined. If not, your church can help you find the best mission agency for you—one that matches your doctrinal and philosophical views of missions, your gifts, and your calling.

If God calls you, He will prepare and empower you. What a glorious calling—to spend your life in partnership with the missionary God, reaching those whom He loves and has chosen!

Robertson McQuilkin is President Emeritus of Columbia International University in Columbia, South Carolina, and served as a church planting missionary in Japan.

JOURNAL WORKSHEET 2

WHERE ARE YOU NOW?

Describe your current involvement in a local church. _____

_____

How is the church benefiting from your involvement in it? _____

_____

How are you presently investing your own finances in local church ministry and in missions? _____

_____

Are you currently supporting a missionary working cross-culturally? If not, who would be the most appropriate person(s) for you to begin supporting now? _____

_____

In what ways do you need to grow as a believer? In what ways do you need to grow in your ministry skills?

_____

_____

What is your church's understanding of the task of missions, and what does your church do to pray for, promote, and finance missions and missionaries? _____

_____

_____

What is your church's expectation for people who want to be missionaries? _____

_____

Is there a particular person in your church you would like to have as a mentor in the process of becoming a cross-cultural servant? _____

_____

With which peer friends could you enter into accountable relationships? _____

_____

With which of your church's missionaries could you discuss your aspirations? _____

_____

What kind of work experience do you have, and what kind of professional skills do you need to develop? _____
_____

Have you asked to serve on (or start) your church's mission committee or review (or help develop) your church mission policy to see that it is up to date? _____

WHAT DO YOU NEED TO DO NEXT?

Is your church offering any short-term trips in which you could participate? _____
_____

How can you best share your decision with your parents and family? _____
_____

When and how will you share your new commitment with your local church? _____

What will your church need to know in order to participate with you? How can you help educate others in your church about world evangelization? _____
_____

If you're living away from home, where will you be actively involved in a local fellowship? How could you serve in a local church? _____

How often do you want to meet with your mentor or spiritual director? _____

When can you form an accountability group? Whom might you include in it? How often do you want to meet? _____
_____

How do you plan to grow in your knowledge of and involvement in world evangelism? _____
_____

With your family, spouse, other Christians you respect, and your advisors at school (as applicable), discuss work opportunities that will complement your plans to become a missionary. Consider your training needs and financial situation.
_____
_____

Whom will you start to support financially now, even if it is only $5 or $10 a month? _____

WHAT WILL THE FUTURE LOOK LIKE?

Where do you envision yourself 5-10 years from now? What do you picture yourself doing? _____
_____

What are the steps necessary to get there? _____

How would you like your church to participate in this venture with you? _____
_____

If you become a missionary, what work experiences do you think might be useful for you to have acquired? _____
_____

What habits or activities do you need to change now in order to be more effective for God in the future? _____
_____

STEP 3: EXPOSURE TO OTHER CULTURES

Steve Hoke

It's been observed that people don't really understand themselves or their culture until they have a chance to step outside their own culture and look back. That distance gives them a fresh perspective. Simply put, that is the great benefit of exposure to other cultures during the early phases of your missionary training: gaining perspective, stretching your vision.

Cultures are neither "right" nor "wrong"; they're just different. Behaviors, language, social systems, cultural values, and worldview all vary depending on your location and the people around you. People who go to live in a culture very different from their own almost universally experience something called "culture shock." That's the stress experienced as a result of losing all the familiar cues from our home culture. Not until we have actually experienced another culture by attempting to live as part of it do we really understand the tremendous differences that exist.

Some are better equipped than others to be "bridge people" between their own culture and the culture in which they are attempting to communicate Christ. God has apparently gifted these individuals with a unique ability to cross cultures. Nevertheless, almost everybody can learn to be more prepared for culture adjustment by deliberately broadening their exposure to other cultures.

Cross-cultural experience cannot be obtained through books, although these will help in your preparation. You need to gain actual experience. It's important that as soon as possible you have an opportunity to live and work in another culture. Even better is a program that permits you to have a series of experiences like this. One experience may not be a true test.

There are many ways this can be done. A number of colleges have a "year abroad" program in which one does a year of study in another country, usually living in the home of nationals. Other colleges offer an inter-term or summer study trip to selected mission fields.

There are myriad short-term missionary experiences available. They vary in length from two weeks to two years. The two-week trips are primarily for exposure and getting your feet wet. Summer mission projects lasting eight to 10 weeks allow you to do ministry, usually using English or a language you may already know. The longer one- and two-year experiences actually place you in ministry roles where you engage in longer-term ministry alongside experienced career missionaries or supervisors. Some groups are specifically designed to place young men and women in short-term ministry experiences cross-culturally; agencies such as Youth With a Mission, Operation Mobilization, and International Teams are notable examples. Others are part of a larger mission program. Some short-termers do specific work. Others go primarily as learners (see the article that follows).

Don't overlook cross-cultural experience in your home country. You'll be surprised at how many people of different cultures live around you. God has brought the unreached peoples to our back door. Visit ethnic neighborhoods in major cities. Consider inner-city summer internships with groups like World Impact, InnerCHANGE, or City Teams. Look for opportunities to work and to serve in ethnic settings. This will sharpen your sense of the delightful differences between cultures and heighten your awareness of the need to build bridges. (See "Why Wait Till You Get There?" on pages 42-43.)

Look through the resources available. Choose specific cultural exposure programs that fit your overall career plan. If possible, choose an agency or project among a people with whom you think you may eventually like to work. For further ideas and resources, read the next two "first person" stories by former short termers, and the guidelines for discovering the best short term for you. Appendix 4 lists numerous mission opportunities you can check out.

MY STORY: TAKE THE SHORT STEP
Short-Term Missions Can Change Your Life
Gene Smillie

It's a great time for short-term missions! There are more opportunities than ever. If you pay attention during your short-term mission trip, you can learn a lot. And these lessons will apply to the rest of your life, paying dividends over and over.

I went on my first short-term mission when I was 20. I spent a year in Colombia. I picked up the language by living with Colombians. Young, single, and adventuresome, I immersed myself in the culture. I came back to the States eager for more cross-cultural experiences and helped start a Chinese church while in graduate school. Later in seminary, I continued my pattern of short-term commitments. I helped in Alaskan Indian villages one summer, spent a year as an inner city church pastor, worked with interracial youth on an army base, and spent time as a prison chaplain. Later I became a career missionary to Côte d'Ivoire, West Africa, where I now serve.

The Attractions

What are the attractions of short-term missionary service? First, the obvious. It's short. You aren't making a lifetime commitment. This is attractive if you aren't sure what you want to do with your life. It's a way to explore God's will—to "get your feet wet" on the mission field and decide whether longer-time service is for you.

Another attraction is the romanticism of it. Going off to New Guinea or Japan or Eastern Europe for a summer is pretty exciting! Short-term missionary work presents a colorful alternative to everyday options. Sometimes it's a matter of getting out of a rut and seeing things from a different perspective. This can be a wonderful catalyst for creative thinking—for shaking up your life and getting on with it.

Short-term mission trips are also attractive if you know you want to work in a cross-cultural setting, but you don't know exactly where or how. A short-term assignment allows you to search out the form and location of your personal missionary calling.

A few generations ago, the "missionary call" was usually a lifelong obligation. This concept has largely been replaced by the idea that God offers us several options—and that we negotiate these options as we go along. Mission boards have adapted to the changing circumstances and attitudes with a variety of missionary service opportunities.

Effectiveness

Mission agencies also understand the cost-effectiveness of short-term missions. Studies show that a disturbing percentage of first-term missionaries don't return for a second term. There's a great loss in investment time and money when someone decides, "I was wrong—God didn't call me to do this." When mission boards allow a person to "try it out first" on a short-term basis, they know they have a solid, long-term missionary if that person decides to return to the field.

What's the actual effectiveness of a short-term missionary? It depends largely on you. Almost everything about your success depends on your attitude. If you expect to serve, you'll have a great ministry. If you expect to be served, the experience will be hard on everyone. This is true in most areas of life, but it's especially true for short-termers.

The work you do on a short-term trip usually contributes in some way to the work being done by career missionaries or national Christians. These people have been in a location for a long time before you get there, and they will be there a long time after you leave. Your time with them is an opportunity for you to learn as well as to serve. Or it can be a time of chafing and impatience. The difference is all in your attitude.

Language and cultural barriers can't be bridged in a few weeks. Of course, if you don't speak the language, the limits of what you can do as a short-term missionary are clear. But cultural barriers—especially subtle ones—are just as real. If you see yourself as a support person, ready to contribute to an ongoing ministry in any way you can, you will make a valuable contribution to any cross-cultural ministry.

Take Heart

Don't be surprised to find yourself facing depression after you arrive on the mission field—particularly if there are significant differences in what you thought you were going to be doing and what you are actually doing. This happens to everybody. It's called culture shock. And as you begin to discover how different the new culture really is from the one you're used to—how superficial the similarities are that you thought you recognized at first—you may begin to feel discouraged.

But take heart. Your very newness will attract some people to you, and they will excuse you for most of your cultural faux pas. Very likely they will laugh with you and forgive cultural "bloopers" that would be unforgivable in others. The depression you experience will give way to acceptance of yourself and your limitations in your new surroundings. You will make good friends, gain a deeper understanding of what God is doing in the world, lighten the load of fellow workers, and see yourself in a new light. Be forewarned. A short-term mission can change your life. But that's partly why you want to go, isn't it?

Gene Smillie is a career missionary with the Christian and Missionary Alliance (C&MA).

MY STORY: WAKE UP, LET'S GROW!
Looking at the World Through Holy Spirit Glasses
Linda Olson

As Prema limped into the room where I was waiting to counsel teenage girls, her brown eyes, full of tears, caught mine. Earlier in the day, I had spoken to her South Indian school group about God's unconditional love. Now our interpreter beckoned Prema to join us and began asking questions. Finally, the interpreter turned to me with the story.

Prema had become a Christian—much to the horror of her devout Hindu family. After beating her severely when they heard of her new faith, they forbade her to attend after-school Bible club meetings. Still, the 13-year-old studied the Scripture whenever possible.

"Should I obey my parents and continue to wear the vermilion dot on my forehead, symbolizing my allegiance to the god Shiva?" she asked me now. "Or should I be bold for Christ, refuse to wear it, and risk another beating?" Then she raised her sari and exposed a small leg, badly swollen from the beating.

Stunned, my heart was filled with sympathy, anger, and confusion. What could I tell her? It seemed nothing in my training had prepared me for this. None of the answers fit. I wanted the right thing for her. I wanted "living for Jesus" to mean goodness and wholeness and love and laughter. Oh, what some parents back home would give to have a daughter so committed to Christ. I fumbled through some answer emphasizing the Lord's love for her and knowledge of her heart. Then I went back to my Indian host family and cried.

A New Shade of Lenses

Until this point, I had been on a short-term mission in India hoping to share the Lord. Now I had to wrestle with the realities of being a Christian and an Indian. I still wanted to share Jesus, but I now knew I would have to take off my own culture-tinted glasses and put on an entirely different shade of lenses.

When God takes us on a journey like mine in India, there is tremendous opportunity for personal growth. Like me, many Christians have a naive view of servanthood. We want to serve where we know we are using our gifts, we know what is required, and we are sure we'll make a difference.

A short-term venture—where the norms of culture and the ways of people are not our own—often shakes our minds and hearts loose from our own assumptions about being a servant for Christ. It can redefine and enrich our view of discipleship and of the Lord we serve. We find ourselves more attuned to God's agenda for the world, less concerned about ourselves, and more open to the leading of the Holy Spirit.

Whether we feel we have nothing to offer or feel we can change the world, a short-term experience puts our personal usefulness to God into a balanced perspective. Few short-termers come claiming to have changed the world in the two weeks or two years they've been gone. But most return with a humble sense that God has used them in His great kingdom gathering. When that humility is in place, the Holy Spirit can do great things through us.

The benefits of a short-term mission go beyond those experienced by the short-termer. When careful planning and training are part of the venture, the receiving community profits greatly. Many ministries around the world badly need the resources we sometimes hoard and even take for granted. They need buildings for shelter and worship. Wells to unite a village. Life-saving technology too long withheld for lack of profit. Evangelism with a creative new twist. Discipleship training from in-depth biblical resources.

This and much more can be offered in loving servanthood by those who come, do a job, and return home to pray. Christians outside our culture have a wealth of gifts for us as well—vision, wisdom, simplicity, commitment—often born of struggle. As we honor the church God is building outside our sociopolitical boundaries, short-term mission can provide a strong network of prayer and care across cultural lines.

A Ripple Effect

Home churches enjoy a tremendous ripple effect from short-termers. The sending process often involves people who might never have given mission a thought. As friends invest personally in the lives of those going and returning in a short time, their own vision for mission is challenged and renewed. In turn, those returning bring a more realistic understanding of the needs of nationals and career missionaries. They come home to lead others in prayer and support.

There is a powerful contagion spread by the Holy Spirit from those who return to the community of believers who sent them. Through the stories and lives of returning short-termers, God calls more and more to join His team of followers—people committed to seeing the Good News extend throughout the world.

After watching several peers make sacrifices for short-term ministry, a young man in my church accepted the Lord's call. He gave up a fine job and entered seminary to prepare for long-term cross-cultural service. A student group that sent several members on a summer mission project began praying regularly and passionately for the community they had visited. Some retirees—after spending a month away investing their professional gifts—returned to recruit others for a program benefiting the homeless right in our own city.

God is using short-term mission to awaken the church worldwide. He is using the Premas of the world to change the hearts of His people and to give them a humble passion for making His name known.

Linda Olson directs training and debriefing for short-term mission teams for InterVarsity Christian Fellowship.

DISCOVER THE BEST SHORT-TERM MISSION FOR YOU

Steven C. Hawthorne

You have an "option overload" problem in missions. Hundreds of mission agencies have opportunities. Many of them want you—or someone like you. And yet each of them is different. Which one is right for you? Which one will best fulfill God's call on your life? I've learned to take note of six decision areas which need to come together for the best missions "fit." Everyone works through them in a different order and in a unique way.

The sequence in which you consider each area, however, makes a great difference. For example, someone who assumes he or she will go overseas for the summer (term) to play basketball (talent) with a sports ministry (team) may or may not then be able to choose between going to Mexico City or to the Muslims in Indonesia (target).

Switch those priorities to spending a summer (term) among Muslims in Indonesia (target), and you may find yourself doing an entirely different ministry with a very different team.

What are *your* priorities? How flexible are they? As you read through the following six decision areas, try to identify your priorities. Then complete the Decision Points Checklist on page 52.

1. Target

Consider your target. What need will you touch? To which country will you go? What people? Which city?

For some individuals, targeting is the main event. Perhaps they feel that God has called them to a particular country. Others figure that it is important to go where they are most needed. Others have learned to put their finger on places and people groups which are strategic in light of the big picture of world evangelism.

For example, some persons get their heart set on going to Kenya, and all their other choices follow from that. Others may find themselves interested in the Muslim world. Others "eat and sleep" China.

2. Task

Consider your task. What kinds of activities will you be doing from day to day? What goals will you accomplish?

Some people are open to serve in just about any way. But others start out fixed on a particular job description. You may have your heart set on digging wells, or church planting, or nursing, or doing literacy work, or helping in churches, or playing with orphans, or doing street evangelism, or even building runways in the jungle. Get acquainted with the range of fascinating possibilities. Dream boldly, but beware of spinning scenarios in your mind which are out of reach. Others don't get so excited about novelty. Widen your willingness to serve by accepting a challenge.

3. Team

Consider your team. With whom will you go? What sending group, mission agency, or church? What relationship will you have with national churches? To step into a short term usually means that a team is taking you on. Suddenly, you will be involved in something larger than yourself or your own career. It's really a matter of trust.

Mission agencies or your church will probably accept you, believing that you will contribute to the task God has given them. You need to trust the leadership of that sending body to help guide your service. If you choose your team first, then they will usually be heavily involved in determining your target, task, and term.

Carefully consider several sending groups. Don't get stuck on one mission just because you knew someone who served with them or because you have supported them in the past. Develop some criteria and go shopping.

A large part of your total team is your family and the church which is sending you. Don't leave them out of your decision at any point. Many of them have developed a strategic vision and program of short-term mission trips that are part of their long-term strategy.

4. Talents

Step back and take a good look at yourself. Consider your talents, gifts, and strengths. What spiritual gifts or natural abilities are called for? What do you like to do most? What weaknesses do you have?

Many people start here on the search. There may be something they're good at, like playing guitar or basketball. Some are pleasantly surprised that their special ability can be put to use in missions. Others, however, get trapped by their own gifts and put undue expectations on mission leadership to assign them duties only in areas in which they excel or have interests. They can easily find themselves disappointed and resentful when they are given tasks which do not give them that magic feeling of "self-fulfillment."

Do not get involved in missions, even short-term, if you merely seek to feel satisfied and good about yourself. Missions work is *work*. It is fundamentally service, not self-fulfillment.

The "vacation with a purpose" can be astoundingly devoid of God's purpose. The currents of our self-seeking culture can drift overseas quite easily. It's a subtle tendency. Short-term missions become expensive summer camp, a career-shopping expedition, or an alternate context for personal soul-searching and career searching. Be careful of viewing your short-term mission too narrowly for what it will do for *you*, the short-termer.

On the other hand, try to find something that fits you best. You may not feel that you have much to offer. You do. You may believe that you don't have many well-developed expectations of your time. Silent expectations are the most dangerous. Get in touch with them.

5. Training

Consider your training. What are you equipped or prepared to do?

You may begin the short-term selection process by examining your education, experience, and qualifications. These are worthy considerations, but sometimes a poor place to start. Although you might find something which fits you, you will probably miss several key opportunities because you're limiting your options to your own current abilities.

Be sure to inventory all your qualifications. You may be more prepared than you think! Check to see if different church and mission structures offer training as part of the short-term experience.

Beware of trying to work missions into your schedule only when it seems convenient. It is rarely convenient to change the world.

6. Term

Consider your term of service. How long a commitment will you be making? Are you thinking of just spending a couple weeks, a summer, a semester, or a year? Do you want an option to extend your term? Are you seriously exploring how to spend most of your life overseas should this short term work out well?

Consider how much more you may gain and give if you were to commit yourself for a year or two instead of just a summer. Be wise about severing ties and quitting jobs. You probably shouldn't burn all your bridges. But do keep in mind that short-term missions *is* missions. *Expect* that you'll need to give up something in order to give something. Beware of trying to work missions into your schedule only when it seems convenient. It is rarely convenient to change the world.

DECISION POINTS CHECKLIST

Use these statements to find out how you've already begun to decide which opportunity might be right for you. How certain you are in some areas will influence your decisions in other areas. Read through the entire list and check each statement that reflects most closely your hopes and desires.

	Certain	Some Idea	Unsure
TARGET (the people, city, or country I'll touch):			
I want to work with a particular people or kind of people.			
I already have a particular country or city in mind.			
I want to avoid certain places or kinds of people.			
TASK (the kind of work I'll do):			
I hope to do outreach/evangelistic activities.			
I want to focus my time on the needs of churches.			
I want to be involved in people's physical and social needs.			
TEAM (the organization I'll go with):			
I want to link up with my church or denomination.			
I'm leaning toward one mission agency already.			
I know what kind of organization I want to go with.			
TALENTS (the skills and gifts I'll use):			
It's important to use my special skills and experience.			
The job has to mesh with my known spiritual gifts.			
I want to do things I haven't done before.			
TRAINING (the schooling I have or need):			
I want further training as part of my short term.			
I have professional training which could be used.			
I want to do something that won't freeze my career.			
TERM (the length of time I'll be gone):			
I just have the summer.			
I want something with long-term options.			
I have to set a limit on the length of time.			

Now return to those statements you checked and decide how certain you are about each. In which of the six areas (Target, Task, Team, Talents, Training, Term) do you have the most certainty? The least? Rate how strongly you want each of them to influence your decision-making regarding your short term. In which areas could you use a little more flexibility? In what areas should you probably be more decisive?

FLYING WITH TWO WINGS

The Place of Short-Term Missions

Bill Taylor

My evaluation of short-term missions comes from the perspective of one who definitely supports them. I have led short-term trips in the past, and I encourage most believers to participate in at least one serious short-term missions trip (lasting 1-24 months).

Benefits

I recognize that short-term missions have contributed strongly to God's Great Kingdom Enterprise. In fact, I can think of 10 significant benefits of short-term trips:

1. They provide hands-on, direct contact with cross-cultural missions.

2. They stimulate realistic vision for the global task.

3. They provide an opportunity to see God at work (in one's personal life and on the mission field).

4. They can stimulate significant intercession by driving home the fact that without prayer, little is accomplished.

5. They offer reality therapy for those who see missions with fuzzy, rose-tinted glasses.

6. They can convert a person into a lifelong intercessor or missions mobilizer back home.

7. They can create within those who go a desire to serve more significantly in their home churches—perhaps using newly acquired skills, and generally with a more global perspective.

8. Short-termers can witness the impact they can make through their example, evangelism, discipleship, or the use or transfer of their specific skills. Through their service they strengthen the on-site, long-term ministry.

9. They provide the foundation for their own potential long-term commitment to career missionary service.

10. They bring glory to the Living God through their demonstrated obedience to the Sending Lord.

Shortcomings

In spite of these 10 positive aspects, however, short-term missions also have some shortcomings.

1. Overstated importance. Champions of short-term missions sometimes appear to proclaim that they have found the decisive answer to world evangelization. This attitude can be found in some short-term mission organizations as well as some local churches.

Those who espouse this view suffer from a reductionism of the Great Commission/Great Commandment task before us. They are looking at the world through a straw—reducing the totality to a single option—when what we need is a broader menu of alternatives.

2. Self-aggrandizement. Veterans of short-term trips can tend to pass themselves off as missions experts. Just because they've been on a brief cross-cultural stint or two doesn't mean there's nothing else for them to learn!

3. Ignored national ministries. Short-term leaders sometimes bypass the goals and ministries of existing national churches and mission agencies. They neglect to recognize that short-termers tend to make their greatest impact when their work is integrated into long-range plans and programs.

4. Too short, too expensive. Some short-term trips are just too limited, too short, and too expensive. Often, long-term missions are accused of high cost, low value. For example, you'll hear that it costs too much to keep a North American missionary family in Japan. "Redeploy them or bring them home!" say budget-conscious Christians.

But what about those nine-day, Easter break, "win Russia for Christ" trips? What does it cost to send 30 high school or college students on such a trip? Is that really the best way to use kingdom money?

Instead of sending a dozen people from Boston to Indonesia for two weeks (discount four days for travel, one for sickness, two for tourism), why not develop a really powerful trip to an inner city, Canada, or Mexico—at a fraction of the cost?

5. Exhausted full-timers. Short-term trips can go to the other extreme by overloading a team's schedule. This saps the limited resources of national churches and expatriate missionaries.

When I was in Latin America, I finally reached the point where I was so frustrated by the demands short-term teams made upon me that I said, "Don't send me one more short-termer who can't get around in Spanish!"

6. Limited results. We need to beware of trips that leave little impact or require nothing after their participants return home. Generally, the younger the participants, the less a short-term mission trip will affect their lives and those of others. But if leadership builds into pre-trip training the serious domestic implications of short-term service, then a much better picture emerges.

7. False impressions. Short-term missions may also foster an unrealistic view of the national church and existing missionaries. A short-termer can easily spend a few weeks at a location and return concluding, "Wow! These missionaries sure are lazy. We got up at dawn and slogged it out until midnight, witnessing, building the church, and running Vacation Bible Schools for the kids. But those missionaries did so little!"

I recognize that lazy missionaries do exist. Still, the reality is that the intensity of short-term enthusiasm simply cannot be sustained amid the daily grind of long-term ministry. When I think of most of the missionaries I know, several descriptive terms come to mind. These people are gifted, well-equipped, dedicated, committed for the long term, quietly interceding, doing invisible acts of love, patiently learning the language and culture, and building trust and credibility so the gospel can penetrate with lasting power.

One reason many short-term workers have such positive relationships with national believers is because they're enjoying the benefit of time-tested trust built by the on-site, long-term missionaries.

Overcoming the Limitations

Some short-term groups have been able to avoid most of these problems. Others have not— probably because they have not thought things through adequately or haven't developed their programs in dialogue with existing ministries on that field.

The situation is complicated by some major changes occurring in North America's younger generation. Many of our young people have a low commitment to anything long-term and are suspicious of absolute truth—whether that means Christianity as a system or Jesus Christ Himself. But every aspect of the global missions enterprise has its problems. The key is to recognize our limitations, invite and listen to outside input, and be willing to change for the better.

Balancing Our Efforts

Is our approach wrong? Should we view short terms strictly as forums for experiencing hands-on training, and focus on accomplishing the task of world evangelization through longer-term ministry?

My answer to that valid question is simple: an airplane needs both wings to fly. We need both short-term and long-term missions. Short terms should be seen, at least in part, as hands-on training for missions. I would like to see more specific equipping for short-term missions (including what to do upon returning home) and a much larger percentage of short-termers committing to long-term missionary service.

One mission agency that I really respect has staff missionaries who are totally dedicated to working with short-term teams. Due to this emphasis, the agency has seen a higher percentage of its short-termers go on into long-term missions. Still, they want to double their numbers.

Stressing Long-Term Missions

Remember, most of the thousands of unreached people groups are unreached because it is tough to reach them! The reasons could be geographical, ethnic, political, religious, or a combination of these factors. I'm deeply convinced that these groups will hear the gospel in their mother tongue, will respond in the power of God, and will see vital churches established—primarily through the work of long-term, dedicated missionaries.

This breed of missionary—I call them an endangered species— is composed of people who have committed for the long haul. They will be sent by their churches as well-trained servant-leaders, buttressed by faithful intercessors.

They will learn the language to speak it proficiently. They will study and understand the culture, raise their families in that context, and establish credibility with the people. And they will see our supernatural God at work.

Reaching the unreached will take a new generation of Boomers and Generation X'ers who decide to go for broke and serve God in long-term missions work. They will need to intern with their local churches and get the right training for the task. They will still need to be sent out by their churches, to work on vital teams on the field. They will still need to stay on the field for 10, 20, even 40 years.

Most of these missionaries will fit our "traditional career missionary" profile. But a good percentage of them will also be bivocational, serving as teachers, engineers, entrepreneurs, consultants, health care providers. These tentmakers will also need the qualities describing traditional long-term missionaries.

Money Isn't the Answer

Would it be better stewardship just to send money instead of sending short-term workers? No! That's a cop-out! It's related to the ill-advised strategy I hear discussed in some circles—that we should stop sending colonial missionaries and just support native missionaries or send money! I sense the potential of a further dangerous tendency in the U.S. First we diminish the screening, recruiting, and sending of long-term missionaries and send short-termers instead. Then we cut down on both long- and short-termers and send money instead. Then we send nothing!

This approach appears cost-effective and less painful at first. But it is unbiblical and perilous for the soul of the global church.

Making Changes

Missions in the American church may be in need of some serious reconsideration and revival, but it's far from a lost cause. There's still time to change our short-term missions mentality. We need to take a careful look at the current status of short-term and long-term efforts, talk to each other, and then see where we can develop strategic partnerships or alliances.

Let's use both wings to fly!

Reprinted from *Mission Today '96* magazine, published by Berry Publishing Services.

PUTTING IT ALL TOGETHER
Five Ways to Sort Through Your Options
Steve Hoke

1. Find a friend to help you. People don't do radical things by themselves. And face it: you're doing something radical by going into cross-cultural work! Find a trusted friend or leader in your church who will understand your motives and mission hopes.

2. Stretch out your future on a timeline. This is one way to identify potential roadblocks and conflicting agendas. A well-thought-through timeline will show you when you are attempting a "mission impossible" with utterly unrealistic expectations.

3. Stretch your faith. On the other hand, don't settle for what is merely possible. God may lead you beyond the easy or the obvious. You'll have to trust Him no matter where you go, but prepare yourself for some risk-taking ventures.

4. Face your fears. You may have good cause to worry. Perhaps you fear being single the rest of your life. You might fail miserably and be embarrassed before everyone who supported you. If you dredge up all the fears and look at them in the light, some will still be scary, but you may also get a laugh out of some silly scenarios in your mind. You might be needlessly afraid of being attacked by guerillas. You might have a phobia about getting shots before you go. You may not feel any more courageous after the exercise, but you won't be paralyzed with false impressions.

5. Deal with freedoms. In order to be truly free to choose the right mission opportunity, you may have to give up some of the prerogatives you think are yours. Obey God. It is not a matter of finding something that "fits" you or furthers your career. The real issue is being utterly mastered by Christ. You may need to face up to a mistaken sense of entitlement. Do you somehow believe that God is rigging up the whole world to revolve around your own self-fulfillment?

It is not a matter of finding something that "fits" you or furthers your career. The real issue is being utterly mastered by Christ.

Be prepared to relinquish areas of your future or dreams that you thought were yours to pursue. If you let them go into God's hand, He has promised to give you more than you bargained for. "*Whoever wants to save his life will lose it, but whoever loses his life for Me and for the gospel will save it*," Jesus said in Mark 8:35. Jim Elliot put it this way: "He is no fool who gives what he cannot keep to gain what he cannot lose."

Adapted with author permission from *Stepping Out: A Guide to Short-Term Missions*. Copyright © 1987 by Short-Term Missions Advocates, Inc. All rights reserved.

JOURNAL WORKSHEET 3

WHERE ARE YOU NOW?

Have you ever traveled outside your home country, or lived for more than three months in another culture? _____

_____

What books have you read that describe the differences among cultures? What stood out? _____

_____

_____

Have you ever attended worship services of another ethnic group? What differences stood out? _____

_____

_____

What ethnic or culture groups do you live near that are different from your own? _____

_____

What country or countries do you think you'd like (or feel led) to visit? _____

_____

How long could you afford to interrupt your academic program or current job? _____

_____

WHAT DO YOU NEED TO DO NEXT?

Identify a specific short-term mission trip in which you are interested. _____

_____

_____

Look at your next spring or summer vacation as a time to schedule a two- to eight-week short-term trip. _____

_____

_____

Try a weekend "Urban Plunge" experience to break out of your comfort zone. _____

_____

_____

WHAT WILL THE FUTURE LOOK LIKE?

What ministry skill(s) do you need to work on the most? _____

_____

_____

What area of the world would you like most to experience? To what part of the world do you sense God's direction or urging? _____

_____

_____

STEP 4: BASIC EDUCATION

Steve Hoke

Visualizing a pyramid may help you understand the critical building blocks in your preparation for missionary service. Your basic education serves as the broad base. By that we refer to your formal schooling, which for most will include primary, secondary, and some kind of college/university education. Others of you will prefer after secondary school some kind of vocational training that equips you for specific tasks. In this way, you are building your skill set for the future, which hopefully will dovetail into cross-cultural missions.

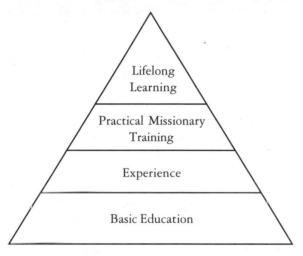

Pyramid of Educational Options

A new face of missions requires a diversity of skills in the cross-cultural force. Here's a sampler: anything in computers, data management, Web-page designs; physiotherapy and occupational therapy certifications; electrical and mechanical maintenance abilities; teaching English as a second language. All of these the Spirit can use.

Further experience, including short-term service, your job(s), church ministry, and relationships, are the building blocks that stretch you higher and at the same time begin narrowing the structure. Practical missionary training and lifelong learning are the blocks that complete the point of the pyramid.

Keeping that picture in mind, let's look at establishing a solid base for your long-term missionary service.

Take an honest look at where you are right now. Is the academic program you're pursuing or have completed adequate for what lies ahead? Can you supplement your basic undergraduate education with other courses? If not, can you find the courses you need? Are they available in your present college or university? Can you find them as distance learning courses, or will you have to change schools?

> *When studied in the context of a Christian college with an integrating core of biblical studies and theology, the liberal arts become the "liberating arts," because they bring all of human inquiry into proper relationship with the freeing truth of Jesus Christ.*

A solid general education is an invaluable foundation for long-term cross-cultural ministry, and it is the educational base most mission agencies prefer. It provides a breadth of understanding and a reference point for all future training. It gives the graduate a general grasp of the liberal arts (especially social and behavioral sciences), natural science, and mathematics.

When studied in the context of a Christian college with an integrating core of biblical studies and theology, the liberal arts become the "liberating arts," because they bring all of human inquiry into proper relationship with the freeing truth of Jesus Christ. Christian students in a secular college or university will have to work extra to make these connections. It's worth the investment. Start where you are. Ask your church or mission agency what courses they suggest or require.

If you're in some stage of undergraduate education: Check your experience for several major components. Most churches and agencies recommend fitting in some courses in cultural anthropology and sociology; if you haven't taken them yet, add them to your schedule in the semesters ahead. And jump at a chance for a course in linguistics!

Also take courses about international relations or regional histories. Macro-economics will broaden your understanding of the critical dynamics pulsing in our world today. Courses in international development will expose you to global inequities that threaten to tear our world apart along ethnic, economic, and political lines.

If you have already completed your undergraduate study: Find the best way to add three major components: (1) biblical training (whether acquired in a non-formal or formal setting), (2) introductions to anthropology and cross-cultural communication, and (3) specialized training in a vocational skill that would give you viability in the global marketplace (see "Options for Learning," pages 59-61).

The new pattern is evident: get your feet wet first; bond with a people; take some first steps in ministry; and then, upon your return to North America, seek further specialized training or retooling.

Most critical to a solid basic education are some foundational courses in Bible and theology and missions. Many churches and agencies will require prospective candidates to have the equivalent of at least one full year of biblical studies and missions. However, given the changing nature of our world and the values of Generation X, many missions are now accepting candidates with less formal biblical and mission education. It's not that less education is needed. It's just that we realize that front-loading too much formal education before a candidate has bonded with a people, ministry, and country may be counterproductive.

You'll need some understanding of the world's religions and of church history. Get the big picture of the world's religions and of church history—particularly missions history. It's true: Those who do not learn from history are doomed to repeat it. The "World Christian Foundations" course developed by the U.S. Center for World Mission in Pasadena, California, is a comprehensive attempt to meet this need in a pattern of half-time distance education that you can

begin right now with your pastor or qualified lay person as a mentor. You can complete a B.A. or earn an M.A. through this course, even after moving to the field. If you can't fit in this heavy a program right away, at least get an overview through the "Perspectives on the World Christian Movement" course or the "Vision for the Nations" video mini-series (see the descriptions and address in Appendix 2).

There's a rich array of educational options from which you can choose: Bible schools, Christian colleges and universities, Christian graduate schools and seminaries, local churches' credit or non-credit courses in biblical basics, and an exploding array of seminars and modules on the Internet. You might even consider studying in another English-speaking country or in the country where you hope to minister. Each of these training options will be described in greater detail in the following article.

In addition, there is a growing number of summer programs, intensive courses, and self-study distance learning courses that can provide you with the basics in Bible study and missions work while you're working full-time or still enrolled in college.

Some agencies and churches will take candidates with a Bible or Christian college education and send them overseas after just a few weeks of orientation. Many missionaries take additional training gradually during their furloughs and study leaves.

Other agencies are designing tracks which place university graduates overseas for two years of initial language and culture learning before bringing them back for specialized Bible and missions training which focuses on the particular people among whom the candidates have chosen to live and minister. In either case, the new pattern is evident: get your feet wet first; bond with a people; take some first steps in ministry; and then, upon your return to North America, seek further specialized training or retooling.

As you can see, churches and agencies are becoming more flexible in the design and timing of basic education programs. Whatever route you take, you will get missionary training—whether that training is formal and done in advance or through the "school of hard knocks." Regardless, the preparation that you receive will make you less vulnerable to premature and painful attrition.

OPTIONS FOR LEARNING
Basic Education for Christian Service
Steve Hoke and Bill Taylor

Five basic formal schooling options are described below. Match the educational mode to your needs, goals, resources, personality, and learning style.

Inside the Undergraduate Classroom

1. Bible colleges. Bible colleges seek to develop Christian leaders who are mature in character and equipped with biblical knowledge. They have had a strong record of turning out men and women who serve as pastors, teachers, missionaries, and leaders in Christian ministry. Seventy-five percent of today's evangelical missionaries received some Bible college training.

At a Bible college, you'll find a large part of the curriculum devoted to biblical studies. You'll learn to study and teach the Bible, how to preach, and how to participate and lead in Christian service. You'll be tutored in practical areas like sharing your faith, planting churches, and nurturing young Christians. You will also find an emphasis on deep spiritual life and on your identity as part of a community of students and faculty committed to loving and serving God.

2. Christian liberal arts colleges and universities. Christian liberal arts colleges specialize in general education programs, seeking to give students a basic grasp of all the academic disciplines from a distinctively Christian perspective. The curriculum is based on the conviction that all truth is God's truth. It links the study of God's creation with the study of God's revelation, helping you to develop a biblical worldview. Studying at a Christian college allows you to integrate biblical training with your academic field of study.

We live in a fragmented society that desperately needs an integrated view of life—a view that connects the fragments and offers meaning to life. Nowhere is this more important than in Christian ministry. No matter what their job description, unless believers possess an integrated, God-centered view of the world, they will have little to offer people of differing cultures. This is the special strength of the Christian liberal arts college.

> *Unless believers possess an integrated, God-centered view of the world, they will have little to offer people of differing cultures.*

3. The unexpected alternative. If you are already out of school, you may benefit from a pattern of study that can adapt to your present responsibilities and move with you to the field if you don't finish before you go. A variety of colleges and universities now offer credit for the "World Christian Foundations" course developed by the U.S. Center for World Mission in Pasadena, California (see the description and address in Appendix 2). The material is equivalent to a traditional year of Bible with mission perspective, but it is packaged for two years of intensive half-time study anywhere under the supervision of a local mentor. It incorporates a wide range of disciplines, from anthropology to hermeneutics, and science to linguistics, around the central theme of God's unfolding purpose. It is as up to date as you can get in terms of the overall scope of God's mission effort and is available for completing a B.A. or earning an M.A. And by enabling you to continue working while you study, WCF can help you avoid the debt trap that ensnares many would-be missionaries.

4. Secular colleges and universities. Secular colleges and universities (private or state) offer superb facilities, diverse academic majors, large research libraries, and a wide range of faculty specialization. Tuition is also greatly reduced for state residents (often about half the cost of private higher education). Active campus ministry organizations can enrich classroom study with discipleship, mentoring, and outreach opportunities.

In North America you have a menu of thousands of these tertiary-level schools. Some are small, tucked into a rural paradise or crammed in the inner city; others are gigantic, again either in rural or urban settings; they range in size from very small to medium to enormous. They can be private (religious or secular in orientation) or public (supported by

> *Don't go into the university without the certainty that God wants you there. On the other hand, we maintain that if the Christian faith does not work at your university, then it surely won't work in another culture.*

state funds). In contrast to many other countries, the U.S. does not have a "national university" that is funded and guided by the federal education industry. Cost factors range across the spectrum, from a relatively frugal cost at certain state universities (perhaps US$9,000 per year for tuition, room, and board) to nearly US$30,000 per year at high-ticket private ones.

One very important point: no missionary sending group will release you if you have a high student debt. At a recent Urbana Student Missions Convention, I did a workshop on missionary equipping. In the question and answer time, a student asked me whether it mattered if he had a high loan debt following college. I said it did, and then I asked him what his debt would be. He blew us out of the room when he said, US$100,000. He was a computer science grad from MIT. I told him to get the best paying job he could find, live like a pauper, pay his debt

in a short time, save money, and then go into missions. He might be able to do this in four years!

How should a Christian decide which secular school to attend if she or he also wants to go into missions? First, seek the counsel of people wiser than you, and that should include your parents and your pastoral team. Listen carefully to them; then pray. Secondly, check out the educational track record of others you know, particularly those who have gone from the university into missions. Third, check out the liberal arts programs that will teach you how to read, think, and write, or the more "marketable" ones that will give you a strong skill set in light of your academic interests. Fourth, investigate the options within your goals, desires, and finances, and then try to visit the schools.

Finally, select a secular school that offers the following for you: the right academic offerings and costs according to your learning capacities and family budget; the presence of vital campus and student-led Christian ministries, coupled by a strong student-loving church with a passion for God and the world, including that campus. We cannot overemphasize the critical role of solid, campus based Christian groups and vibrant, worshiping, intergenerational communities. Never minimize your church experience. In both the campus ministry and church, you will find teachers of God's Word, disciplers and mentors, life friends, and perhaps a husband or wife with the same passionate goals in life.

Some young adults fear they will lose their faith in the secular college or university. To be honest, we have seen that happen, and it hurts; it may have a parallel to the gradual stagnation of faith that can occur in a Christian school where the tough issues are not faced. Don't go into the university without the certainty that God wants you there. On the other hand, we maintain that if the Christian faith does not work at your university, then it surely won't work in another culture. Learn to tell the powerful Christ-story in that university, and you will never forget the mistakes make, the lessons learned, the exhilaration of seeing the Triune God at work in Spirit power! Make friends with the agnostic, the New Ager, the Buddhist, Hindu, Muslim, Marxist (they are still around), whether they be from your own culture or international students. Learn to listen to their story, and thus you gain credibility that allows you to share with them the Great Story and the way it has bisected your own life.

Moving on to Graduate Courses

5. Christian graduate schools and seminaries. Christian graduate schools are primarily concerned with biblical study and professional training for areas of Christian ministry. Graduate schools equip you with a specialty at a professional level. You can hone your professional skills in journalism, cross-cultural studies, health care, TESL, and so on.

Seminaries offer pastoral preparation in areas such as missions, theology, spirituality, preaching, Christian education, and church

The most critical issue is whether you can develop the character qualities and practical ministry skills demanded in the cross-cultural setting.

planting. Adequate professional training has become increasingly crucial for prospective long-term missionary candidates. Some believe seminary training is mandatory for the cross-cultural church planter. But the most critical issue is whether you can develop the character qualities and practical ministry skills demanded in the cross-cultural setting.

Missions involves many skills in interpersonal relations, networking and resource linking, cross-cultural communication and

counseling, mentoring, and facilitating. However, increasingly, cross-cultural, long-term servants in the "less reached world" need legitimate vocations or skills for visas, as well as to "ground" ministry in the various marketplaces.

Each seminary has its own distinctive style and emphasis. Some are known for training gifted preachers. Others are known for their counseling or mission programs. Still others specialize in urban ministry or international studies. If you attend seminary, the school and its faculty will have a powerful impact on you and on the shape of your theological persuasions. Select a seminary that's compatible with your particular calling or gifting.

A Rich Phase

Whatever avenue of training or study you choose, it can be a rich phase of your life. It's a time when lifelong friends are made and life partners are often found. Surrounded by like-minded teachers and students, you'll find freedom and support to test your calling and refine the direction of your life.

JOURNAL WORKSHEET 4

WHERE ARE YOU NOW?

Does your present curriculum and/or your past educational experience give you an adequate basic education, including some Bible and some social science? If it does, explain how. _____

_____

_____

If it doesn't, map out the courses you need. _____

_____

_____

How strong is your grasp of the Bible, its structure, its message, its origins, and its content? _____

_____

_____

How and when will you investigate the intensive summer courses or distance learning options available? _____

_____

WHAT DO YOU NEED TO DO NEXT?

If your present education is not adequate, what steps do you need to take to supplement it or to switch to a more beneficial program? _____

_____

_____

What extension/distance learning courses or summer intensive courses will you explore? Which churches or agencies should you contact? (See the Resources section in Appendix 2.) _____

_____

_____

How can you arrange this new course of study? What help will you need? From whom? _____

_____

_____

WHAT WILL THE FUTURE LOOK LIKE?

If you complete the program(s) you're proposing, how will this prepare you to move ahead with advanced training at home or overseas? _____

_____

_____

How well prepared will you be to think about the world, as its social and economic makeup continue to change?

_____

_____

_____

Phase 2:
Getting There – Linking

Step 5: Church and Agency Contact and Candidacy

Step 6: Ministry Assignment Search

Step 7: Hands-On Missionary Training

STEP 5: CHURCH AND AGENCY CONTACT AND CANDIDACY

Steve Hoke

The next critical step to consider (and the point at which many prospective candidates get sidetracked or detoured) is how you'll get there. Will you serve with a specific mission agency, church, or denomination?

Romans 10:15 asks, "How can they preach unless they are sent?" Experience shows that those who are sent within the framework of a mission agency or church denomination are most likely to be effective, long-term missionaries. The wisest sending churches are developing strategic alliances with established field based teams or agencies.

Begin with input from your home church. By now you should have a good feel for the missions heart and vision of your own church. Is their vision compatible with yours? If you're a member of a denomination, get information about your denomination's mission first.

Continue with the mission agency you know best. What agency or agencies do your family, missions committee, and pastor recommend that you consider? Do they have a relationship with one or several agencies? What do you know about the church's missionary sending process?

Check out the organization's theology, model of ministry, vision, and leadership. Are their views compatible with yours? If so, this is a natural place to start. If not, it's wise to continue to explore until you find at least a few other agencies with whom you find compatibility on the major issues.

Take a wider look around. There are thousands of strong churches and over 700 North American agencies with a wide span of cross-cultural ministry interests. They range in size from those with thousands of missionaries to those with just a handful.

Some minister all over the world. Others work only in one country. Many have broad, holistic ministries—from relief and development to church planting to theological education. Others have very specific ministries such as literature distribution, church planting, or leadership development. Many are inter-denominational; they have on their staff men and women from many different denominations.

Some agencies are deeply involved in church planting, while others may consider it their major role to serve the existing church. Some target specific peoples, such as Muslims or Native American peoples. Some focus on the vast "unevangelized" world. Others have broader geographic involvement.

Check out the key source of agency information—the most recent edition of *The MARC Mission Agency Handbook: North America Protestant Ministries Overseas.* This triennial publication catalogs the more than 700 agencies in North America and describes their doctrinal emphasis, focus of ministry, size, and the types of missionaries they look for. Agencies are cross-listed by countries and type of ministry.

> *Experience shows that those who are sent within the framework of a mission agency or church denomination are most likely to be effective, long-term missionaries.*

Call, e-mail, or write to agencies. Direct your inquiries to the candidate coordinator or director of personnel. Someone in each agency will be glad to explain their distinctive procedures, from prerequisites to application to appointment. The important thing is that you contact several agencies as soon as you have a handle on some of the questions to ask.

Local church and regional mission conferences are a fantastic opportunity to meet personally with mission agency representatives. The Urbana Student Missions Convention, in particular, is a prime opportunity to meet representatives from dozens of agencies involved in the full range of ministry, from evangelism and church planting to mission aviation, medical ministry, and micro-enterprise development. This national conference is held every three years on the campus of the University of Illinois and is coordinated by InterVarsity Christian Fellowship. The next Urbana Convention is scheduled for December 27-31, A.D. 2000.

The initiative lies with *you.* Remember, God wants you to be in a growing relationship with Him. He has a distinctive purpose for your life.

That purpose involves providing His guidance to take you exactly where He wants you to be. That place is worth seeking in faith.

Don't let anyone tell you that investigating or seeking is "unspiritual." Scripture encourages the right kind of seeking, and that includes investigating ministry roles and the gifts necessary to fill them. See 1 Timothy 3:1 and 1 Corinthians 12:31.

For some more thoughts on churches and agencies, check out the next article.

HOW TO CHOOSE
A SENDING CHURCH OR AGENCY

Bill Taylor

Dear Raquel and David,

Here I am again, attempting to do a better job at answering the great question you lobbed at me during the missions conference. You are right in wanting to be careful when you consider which mission "team" you'll join. From the start, let's clarify some really crucial items.

Who sends the missionary? There's no question in my mind that the local church does that. Too many missionaries feel that their agency sends them out. They want their church to bless and support them, but not to truly send them, with all the responsibility this entails. Bad mistake! You can thank God you're in a church with a heart for its city as well as for the world, and with a pastoral team that shares those powerful core values.

As we discussed the other night, there are two major ways of getting to and staying on the field long-term. One is for your church alone to send you and attempt to provide the critical field components: shepherding, strategizing, supervising, and support system. Few churches can really do all these things well.

I'm encouraged that your church has chosen the second option: to enter into a covenant relationship with an experienced mission agency which will work with you and the church to provide these field elements. You shouldn't leave home without having that settled!

Remember that joining a mission agency is similar to marriage (though it's not always for life). It's a serious, long-term, mutual commitment with heavy implications. Joining the right "ministry family" means time spent "courting"— getting to know each other, evaluating the fit, knowing that God is guiding both parties into this relationship. It's crucial that you be totally united on this. Yet remember, *no perfect ministry exists!*

Now, what specific items should you look for in mission agencies? Here are some guidelines to point you along the path.

1. What are their core spiritual commitments? Each church or agency will have a written affirmation of their beliefs. Many times this is called a *doctrinal statement.*

Strong missiology is rooted in biblical theology. You'll want to work with a team that shares your foundational belief system. So check out that doctrinal statement!

Is the statement general (and probably fairly short) or detailed and specific? Some people feel comfortable in organizations that are very specific about what they believe; others prefer to work where there is broad latitude based on general evangelical orthodoxy.

> *Too many missionaries feel that their agency sends them out. They want their church to bless and support them, but not to truly send them, with all the responsibility this entails.*

Be sure you agree with your agency on some of the more controversial issues. For example, if you prefer a charismatic expression of theology, ministry, and worship, but the agency you're considering doesn't endorse that option, then move on.

2. What's their history? How did they get started? How have they changed? How have they adapted to meet the challenges of the new millennium ahead? Who have their key leaders been? Are any of them still around and available to talk with you? When you get a sense of team history, you can understand where the organization is and where it will probably go tomorrow. Get comfortable with this history.

3. How does the church or agency articulate its purpose, goals, and objectives? This information will be derived from the group's history, but you should also be able to find some clear statements that indicate where they're heading.

Consult others "in the know" to make sure these core values really work in practice! You'll want to work with a team whose goals you respect and share.

To determine whether the agency works strategically, ask whether it has a short-range and a long-range plan. How do they evaluate their progress? Learn about their decision-making process. Is it centralized, democratic, personalized, home or field based, elected, or what? What role does the national church have in evaluating the effectiveness of the mission? Does it have personnel from a diversity of cultures and nations?

You may also want to investigate what kind of team ministry they encourage and what kind of participation they invite from staff. How sensitive is leadership to new ideas? How direct and open are they in resolving conflict?

4. To what types of ministry are they particularly committed? Do they have a strong and holistic view of the Great Commission? Is their ministry based on kingdom values? Do they say they serve the church—and do they really do so? Are they exclusively "into" unreached peoples in the 10/40 Window, or do they have a broader perspective of global need? Will they place you in a ministry that provides a good "gift match," or do they want you to be willing to do anything?

Again, the "right" answers to these questions will depend on the direction and priorities God has given you. Make sure you really can work with the ministry perspective of your potential mission agency. If you want to plant churches, but the organization you join only does evangelism and disciple-making, then *you* will have to change!

A subset of this question deals with geography. Raquel and David, you two have expressed a desire to plant churches among unreached peoples, so be sure the agency you choose is one that works in those kinds of contexts. Some of us *seem* called to a specific country or a particular ministry. We have to search for the right fit, and everything doesn't always come together! But we can try.

5. What kind of care do they provide, both prior to departure and on the field? Be leery of the agency that says something like, "Well, to be honest, our missionaries really don't need much pastoral care. They're all pretty strong, committed Christian leaders."

Related to this is the organization's concept of the family and view of the education of your children. How flexible are they in terms of gender issues and roles for the wife? How comfortable are you with the schooling options they offer your kids?

6. How do they handle finances and support raising? Do they require you to raise all or part of your support? How will they help you in this? What is their administrative cost, and how is it raised?

Will they allow or expect you to provide partial support for yourself on the field—through teaching or a business venture, for instance? What's their housing policy? Can you own your own home "at your own risk"?

Are they a reputable organization, with open accounting and financial management? Can you respect the lifestyle of their missionaries and home staff?

7. What is their relationship to your church as well as the national church? How much are they willing to work with your church leadership as they put together the ministry package for you?

Obviously, if you plant the gospel among a totally unreached people group, *you* hope to see the first national church. But in most countries, there already exists some kind of national group of believers. How has the agency you're considering transferred responsibility and authority to the national churches? What role do these churches have in the placement and supervision of expatriate missionaries?

8. What can you discern about the missionaries' lifestyles and unwritten rules? This is a tough one to discover, but it's really important. As a friend of mind says, "Turn on your spiritual radar system" to find this out. Ask wives and missionary children how they feel about the mission and why. Investigate the lifestyles of

WHAT THE SENDING GROUP (CHURCH/MISSION) WANTS TO KNOW ABOUT YOU!

Bill Taylor

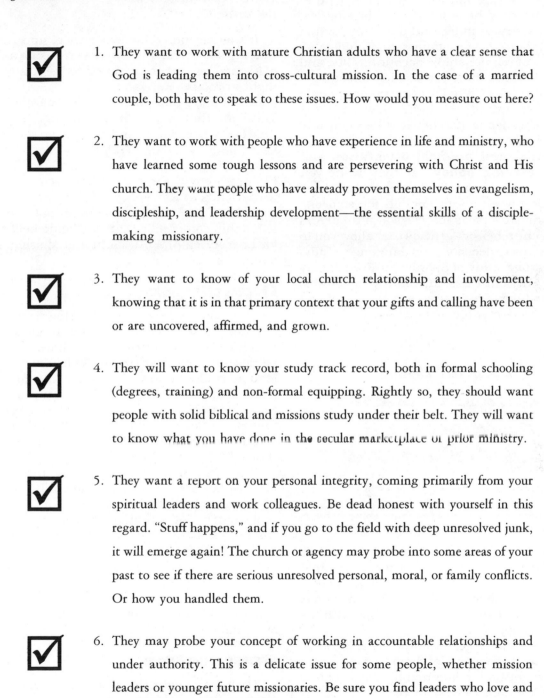

1. They want to work with mature Christian adults who have a clear sense that God is leading them into cross-cultural mission. In the case of a married couple, both have to speak to these issues. How would you measure out here?

2. They want to work with people who have experience in life and ministry, who have learned some tough lessons and are persevering with Christ and His church. They want people who have already proven themselves in evangelism, discipleship, and leadership development—the essential skills of a disciple-making missionary.

3. They want to know of your local church relationship and involvement, knowing that it is in that primary context that your gifts and calling have been or are uncovered, affirmed, and grown.

4. They will want to know your study track record, both in formal schooling (degrees, training) and non-formal equipping. Rightly so, they should want people with solid biblical and missions study under their belt. They will want to know what you have done in the secular marketplace or prior ministry.

5. They want a report on your personal integrity, coming primarily from your spiritual leaders and work colleagues. Be dead honest with yourself in this regard. "Stuff happens," and if you go to the field with deep unresolved junk, it will emerge again! The church or agency may probe into some areas of your past to see if there are serious unresolved personal, moral, or family conflicts. Or how you handled them.

6. They may probe your concept of working in accountable relationships and under authority. This is a delicate issue for some people, whether mission leaders or younger future missionaries. Be sure you find leaders who love and understand the qualities of the younger generation. But are you teachable? Do you have a sacrificial spirit?

single missionaries. How sensitive is the agency to the issues, needs, and concerns of singles, as well as to those of married couples and families?

Ask the organization's leaders what kind of expectations they have for their missionaries. Does the agency or individual offer any kind of job description? Who commits to fulfilling it? What types of relationships, accountability, and reporting formats does the agency encourage, require, or provide? What mutual commitments are made regarding furlough? How does the agency encourage leadership development and lifelong learning?

9. What's their pre-field orientation and language-learning policy? If they want you there only for one week of orientation, keep looking. One week is not enough for someone who's heading overseas for years at a time. And be wary of churches or agencies that allow you to make your own decisions on language study. Basic language study of Spanish or French may take one year, but Russian, Chinese, or Arabic will always take *at least* two years! Some of you will have to learn two new languages!

Remember that there are no perfect organizations. Be realistic. Beware of rapid decisions and "love affairs" with a particular team. The post-honeymoon blues can be fierce!

Finally, remember that there are no perfect organizations. Be realistic. Beware of rapid decisions and "love affairs" with a particular team. The post-honeymoon blues can be fierce! And be sure that your church is happy with the choice of agency.

Take the time to get to know organizations. Find out about them and let them find out about you. It's a mutual relationship; the agencies ultimately want God's best for you.

As I reread this long letter, I hope it's not overkill. Relax, friends! Work with God in this process. And don't forget that we—your family, friends, and church—are on your side!

With respect and love,
Bill

CALLING FOR THE RETURN OF THE RARE BREED
The Long-Term Servant
Bill Taylor

It was an incredible experience, and I knew that my son David and I were witnessing a piece of history, as well as peering into the future that night in Kijabe, Kenya.

David and I had finished participating in the Third International Conference on Missionary Kids (we're both MKs), and we were on the way to visit the Missionary Training College, which trains Africans for cross-cultural service, in Eldoret, Kenya. En route we stayed overnight with friends at Rift Valley Academy, a large MK school in Kijabe. We providentially sat in on the fellowship conference that was being held there for East Africa AIM (Africa Inland Mission) missionaries.

A Legacy of Longevity

That night AIM celebrated with gratitude the decades of service of six veteran missionary couples who were retiring. They shared gripping stories—of their first trek to Africa, of the Mau Mau Rebellion years, of what it meant to be pioneer missionaries, of the changes experienced in their lifetimes. Now they faced the uncertainty of retirement in a far-off land, the country that had issued their passports— "home."

But what astonished me was the service longevity of these men and women. It *averaged* 45 years per person! Among the 12 of them, they represented 540 cumulative years of service, which translates into 6,480 months, 28,080 weeks, 197,100 days! What a legacy! It was an honor for us to observe these veterans and think of that glorious day in the Throne Room of the Lamb when they will celebrate with African believers from different tribes, languages, and even nations.

Glimpse of the Future

That same night the AIM multinational missionary force welcomed 25 single, short-term missionaries from the U.K. who were dedicating two years to teach God's Word in Kenyan schools. They were young, bright, committed, cross-cultural servants, dressed in British funky styles, who would have to minister only in

English (not the mother tongue of their pupils), since their time was limited.

Were we peering into the future? Was the day of the veteran, the "lifer," the really long-term missionary, *over?*

U.S. statistics in 1996 indicated that we were sending some 33,074 fully-supported long-term missionaries (serving more than 4 years); 6,562 short-term missionaries (serving from 1 year up to 4 years); 507 non-residential missionaries (based not in their country of service but traveling there regularly); 63,995 short-termers (2 weeks up to 1 year); and 1,336 bivocational associates (sponsored or supervised tentmakers).

There are some things that can only be done by the long-term missionary. That's why we still need many more "lifers."

That gives us a total, including all categories, of 105,474 missionaries. Only 31% are long-termers, and 67% are short-termers. The remaining 2% are the tentmakers and non-residential missionaries.

Why have the scales tipped from the older decades, when the overwhelming number of missionaries were "lifers"? A number of reasons come to mind:

• God does different things at different times of history.
• Our society has changed.
• Different needs have emerged.
• The amazing Two-Thirds World missionary movement has exploded on the scene.
• Today's missionaries come from many countries (not just the U.S. and Canada).
• Our culture reflects a new mentality of lower institutional commitment and higher mobility—hence a "shopping mall" mindset that wants it now but also wants the freedom to change its mind tomorrow.

A Continuing Need

Do we really *need* more long-term missionaries? Couldn't we send out hundreds of thousands of short-termers to complete the task of world evangelization? Wouldn't we get a better investment return on our missionary dollar if we supported fewer North American career missionaries and countless thousands of "native missionaries"?

No! It would be neither biblical nor right to phase out the career servants. What's more, as Christian stewards, we reject the cost-effectiveness mentality of getting more missionary "bang" for your buck.

Lest I be judged as anti-short-term, let me clarify. I fully support, personally and financially, short-term missionaries. The Holy Spirit is using them in marvelous, unique ways, particularly if they work in the field in partnership with established churches or veteran missionaries or qualified national leaders. I respect them for their commitment, knowledge, skills, and servant spirit.

I'm for short-termers. But there are some things that can only be done by the career, long-term missionary. That's why we still need many more "lifers."

Distinctives of Long-Term Service

1. Short-termers can love the national people, but it takes the patient work of the long-term servant to learn the people's "heart language" with excellence. Speaking the language in which the people think, dream, sing, argue, and love opens the door to their hearts and souls in an irreplaceable way. The story of Jesus then flows over a bridge of integrity-built relationships.

2. Short-termers can minister effectively during their limited stay, but it's the longer-term servant who, over time, builds relationships of confidence with the people, understands their culture, and sensitively contextualizes the gospel within that vibrant reality.

3. Short-termers may leave a legacy, but the one who stays longer is able to invest over the years in lasting discipleship and leader development. He or she will witness the rise and expansion of churches, the emergence and training of new leaders, and then the transfer of responsibility and authority.

4. Short-termers are missionaries also; but it is the long-term missionary who can invest in the new generation of the Two-Thirds World (or European or Russian) missionary force—the veterans with experience will invest in their new partners.

5. Married short-termers experience brief or partial family immersion in culture and ministry. The career family, by contrast, experiences the joy of birthing and raising their family in another culture, with all its positives and negatives.

6. Short-termers can faithfully distribute copies of the Word of God, but it takes a long-haul servant to translate the Scriptures and prepare them for publication and distribution.

7. The most recent Population Data Sheet reports 5.8 billion people in our world, with only 1.175 billion in the so-called "more developed" world and 4.6 billion in the "less developed" world. In the providence of God, the growth of the church is not contingent on degrees of socio-economic development. Rather, it comes from the sovereign movement of the Spirit and the obedience of God's sensitive children. The 1997

The church will be established among unreached peoples primarily by the long-term missionaries who are willing to invest at least 10 to 20 years of their lives—perhaps even to give their lives— for the sake of reaching their corner of the world with the gospel of Christ.

edition of *Operation World*, by Patrick Johnstone, reveals another dimension: a world of some 11,874 unreached people groups in our global family, and about half of them in the unevan-gelized/unreached world. And they are un-reached in part because they are tough to reach.

How will these people groups hear the gospel in their own language and within the context of their own cultural reality? Through obedient servants.

Yes, the short-termers can invest a brief segment of their lives—perhaps showing the "Jesus" film, perhaps sharing their testimonies, perhaps helping gather research or assisting long-term workers in many other creative ways. But the church will be established among unreached peoples primarily by the long-term missionaries who are willing to invest at least 10 to 20 years of their lives—perhaps even to give their lives—for the sake of reaching their corner of the world with the gospel of Christ.

Forget the Statistics: Meet Some Real People

I recently spoke on the phone with Carl, a dear friend who is currently on home leave from his Middle Eastern field of service. Carl and I met during the years I taught at Trinity International University. I saw him mature in Christ and marry Sally, an equally faithful disciple. I witnessed their profound commitment to Christ and their willingness to obey Him in cross-cultural ministry.

From the start, Carl and Sally were "lifers" with their faces set toward the Muslim world. Neither came from an evangelical background. Both had come to Christ during their university years. They completed their formal biblical studies, joined a solid mission agency, raised their support from committed churches with which they established relationships, then moved to the Middle East. Was it easy to leave their beloved families? Not at all! But they left anyway because of the impelling Spirit of God.

Carl and Sally have now lived for over nine years in their adopted culture. They went to the field with one young son; their family has since grown to include two more boys.

Has it been simply marvelous and wonderful in the new country? Not on your life! But I shall never forget something Carl said years ago.

"I plan to live my life in the Middle East," he told me. "After the two required years of Arabic study, I know it will take me another eight years to gain high proficiency. But that's what it takes. And my desire is to know God's Word released with power. I also plan to study the Koran deeply in order to understand my Muslim neighbors."

Carl and Sally and their three boys. A longer-term missionary family.

Then there's Doug. He dropped by the house yesterday. We had a rich time together. He's a recently married, long-term cross-cultural servant who's committed to Poland. Doug's objective is to see new churches established, to see leaders trained in the context of their ministry as well as in the emerging evangelical seminary in Poland. He went out single, and God recently led him to a young woman who shared the same passion and who served initially in Romania.

Doug jolted me with the statement, "You know, Bill, I didn't go to Eastern Europe to save souls; I went to know

God better. And that is what has happened to me through the long and hard work of learning the language, studying the culture, and understanding the people of Poland. I know God better."

That's similar to the strong words another friend of mine says: "The purpose of missions is not to fulfill the Great Commission. Rather, it is to increase the number of people on earth who worship the one true and living God with reverence and awe, giving Him the glory He deserves."

Sure, a short-termer could say the same thing. But there's really nothing like experiencing this goal and outcome over the course of years, decades, a lifetime of service.

The purpose of missions is not to fulfill the Great Commission. Rather, it is to increase the number of people on earth who worship the one true and living God with reverence and awe, giving Him the glory He deserves. →

The Payoff

Is there a special payoff, a compensation for long-term (even "lifer") missionary service? Let me answer it in the words of another colleague of mine. "We have a job that's extremely dangerous and extremely costly, with little compensation, except the satisfaction of obeying Christ among the people of the world in a distant and strange country."

Also, as the church in a given area is born and grows and learns to reproduce itself, the long-term missionary has the satisfaction of watching the whole process, analogous to observing a baby born into your family, then witnessing the growth and development of that child into its own reproductive maturity. These, then, are some of the benefits of the long-term missionary.

My mom and dad are lifers who went to Costa Rica in 1938. They still serve cross-culturally as Hispanic church planters (now in their "home" country) at the ages of 84 and 88.

My wife and I served 17 years as missionaries to Latin America. Our three children were born there, studied in a trilingual school, and watched with us as the book of Acts came alive in the Guatemalan church of which we were a part. That church first met us as foreign missionaries, but when we left Latin America, they sent us out as part of their own missionary force!

Did we have tough times and wonder what was happening to us? Of course! But we hung in for a longer haul. We wouldn't trade our experience. These are just a few of the benefits of longer-term missionary service.

Is the career missionary a vanishing species in our North American society? Some might suggest so, but I'd cry out, "No!" And I invite thousands of select short-termers to convert their rich experience into long-term cross-cultural service. You may feel that life is just too indefinite or that global socioeconomic trends are too discouraging, and we just can't plan that far in advance. The answer there is quite clear: no believer knows the future. But if you can plan for short-term service in an uncertain world, that experience equips you to aim for a long-term ministry of at least 5-10 years. You might even go for 45 years!

Commit for the long term. Let God direct you to a life of cross-cultural ministry that, while deepening your reliance on Him and your relationship with Him, brings many more people into the rainbow coalition of white-hot worshipers surrounding the Lamb on the throne!

Some Key Questions and Issues

If you want to be a career missionary, what elements should you keep in mind? Here's a checklist:

1. What are your deepest motives for desiring missionary service?

2. In what ways have you been tested spiritually?

3. What aspects of the global mission task seem to require longer-term missionaries?

4. What does your interest and gift inventory report? What do you enjoy doing, and what are you naturally skilled at doing?

5. What kinds of specific education and training do you need in order to channel your interests and sharpen your skills/gifts? How long might this take?

6. In what ways is your church committed to these same passions? How can you be an integral part of the life of your church as you follow in obedience your path to the nations of the world?

JOURNAL WORKSHEET 5

WHERE ARE YOU NOW?

What missionaries have you met from whom you'd like to learn more? How can you contact them? _____
_____
_____

Does your church have an active missions program? If so, who are the key people who could tell you more about the agency or agencies your church is related to? Schedule a meeting with them. _____
_____
_____

If you're a member of a church denomination that has a sending agency, how can you and/or your church leaders contact them? _____
_____

What city, nation, and unreached people group(s) is your church targeting? _____
_____

In what country would you like to serve, or what unreached people(s) would you like to play a part in reaching? _____
_____

Do you have friends who are also looking to make contact with an agency? What are they discovering? _____
_____
_____

WHAT DO YOU NEED TO DO NEXT?

When will you check out your church's mission program? Set a date or deadline and write it here. _____
_____

If you're a member of a denomination, set a date for contacting the candidate secretary or writing for information.
_____

When will you look at other agencies beyond your church or denomination, if necessary? _____
_____

WHAT WILL THE FUTURE LOOK LIKE?

What criteria will you and your church use to determine which mission agency is the best "fit" for you? _____
_____
_____

What limitations on debt, family size, theology, etc., do you need to be aware of in relating to an agency? _____
_____
_____
_____

STEP 6: MINISTRY ASSIGNMENT SEARCH

Steve Hoke

The next two steps—seeking out the place where God wants you to serve and getting hands-on training—overlap with the step of finding the right agency. Each one influences the others. So steps 5, 6, and 7 should all be tackled simultaneously, as a single unit.

It's necessary to ask God specifically about the *role* you are to play in seeing Him plant a strong, vibrant church in a part of the world where Jesus is not known.

Although this workbook has been designed with varied roles in mind, the profile on pages 26-27 highlights one of the roles most essential to the decade ahead. Church planting remains a critical role. There are nearly two billion people in some 6,500 people groups who live beyond the

---

Avoid making quick judgments or being too easily attracted to (and distracted by) "easy" jobs or the prospect of some "exotic" adventure.

---

reach of God's tender mercies—with little or no culturally relevant Christian witness. Unless many Christians, from many places, go specifically to these unreached peoples with an understanding of their language, their culture, and their needs, no new church can be established among them.

But other roles are needed too. On page 74 we have listed several other missionary tasks which focus on and supplement church planting. We've also listed the types of preparation required for them. Maybe there's a certain role that fits you, your training, your experience, and your gifts. If God has specifically equipped you to serve as a teacher to MKs, for example, then go ahead! There's no need to feel guilty about filling a much-needed support role.

Regardless of what you now see as the task to which God is calling you, you'll find it extremely helpful to think about and focus on a particular

people group. Ask your church or agency to help you study a people group, or perhaps several people groups which occupy the same region—or the vast unreached cities of our globe.

Look for evidence of God's leading: a match between your natural abilities, learned skills, and spiritual gifts and the characteristics and situation of the people. Avoid making quick judgments or being too easily attracted to (and distracted by) "easy" jobs or the prospect of some "exotic" adventure. Hawaii is no longer unreached. Neither are San Diego, Cancun, or Monte Carlo.

Patiently wait for God's leading to be reinforced by other indicators or "wisdom signs." Prayer, "divine appointments" (those uncanny times when God providentially leads across your path just the person you need to talk to), confirming spiritual counsel, an overriding sense of His peace, and even circumstances, to some extent, can serve as wisdom signs.

The Apostle Paul was "called" into full-time ministry at his conversion on the Damascus road (Acts 9), but he wasn't "sent" out until he was commissioned by the Antioch church in Acts 13, a number of years later. If Paul could wait for confirmation, so can you. "Calling" and "timing" are two crucial but very different issues to keep balanced.

What if you don't know where you're supposed to go or have no geographic preference? What if you don't know of any unreached people groups? The suggestions listed below were gathered from others who have faced the same predicament.

1. Tune into the clues around you. Learn about the particular people group or geographical focus your home church emphasizes. Pray regularly for specific unreached people(s), nations, and cities listed and described in *Operation World*, the best geographical prayer digest. Be aware of the people God leads into your life (divine encounters), friends who have a similar burden, international students you encounter who are all from a certain part of the world, or a growing concern about a special people to whom God clearly indicates He wants to lead you.

2. In your journal, keep track of insights or strong interests as they develop. Each week, review what you've written,

THE MISSIONARY PREPARATION MATRIX

There are thousands of unreached people groups with no Christian witness. Each requires a well-trained team of church planting missionaries. But other roles are needed, too. In the chart below, we have tried to show the different kinds of training needed for different tasks.

TYPES OF MISSION ROLES/ CAREERS	STEP 1 Spiritual Formation	2 Body Boost	3 Exposure	4 Basic Education	5 Agency Contact	6 Assignment Search	7 Hands-On Training	8 Apprenticeships	9 Lifelong Learning	10 Finishing Strong
Agriculturist	X	X	X	X	X	*	*	?	X	X
Church Developer/ Church Renewal Specialist	X	X	X	X	X	X	X	X	X	X
Church Planter	X	X	X	X	X	X	X	X	X	X
Community Development Worker	X	X	X	X	X	X	X	*	X	X
Evangelist/Discipler	X	X	X	X	X	X	X	X	X	X
Field Researcher	X	X	X	X	X	X	X	X	X	X
Health Specialist	X	X	X	X	X	X	X	*	X	X
Journalist	X	X	X	X	X	X	*	—	X	X
Medical Doctor	X	X	X	X	X	X	*	X	X	X
Mission Counselor	X	X	X	X	*	X	*	*	X	X
Mission School Teacher/ Administrator	X	X	X	X	*	X	X	—	X	X
Nurse/Pharmacist/ Lab Technician	X	X	X	X	X	*	X	—	X	X
Pastoral Mentor/Coach	X	X	X	X	X	X	X	X	X	X
Pilot/Technician	X	X	X	X	X	*	*	X	X	X
Secretary/Admin. Asst.	X	X	—	X	X	X	—	—	X	X
Tentmaker	X	X	X	X	*	X	*	—	X	X
Theological Educator	X	X	X	X	X	X	X	—	X	X

* Specific to technical skill

? Requirements are variable, not specific

reflect on it, and see if any patterns, divine encounters, or contacts with a particular people in a particular part of the world have emerged. Be attentive, as well, to what God may be teaching your church about their missions focus.

3. Be open to traveling and visiting regions within the vast unreached world.

4. Interview missionaries and international students who have come from similar regions or who are from a particular people group. Learn all you can. Keep track of your insights.

5. Be up-front about a call that conflicts. If you sense a growing call to a people group other than those emphasized by your home church, it's time for intensive prayer and sensitive communication. Take the initiative to share clearly and honestly with your leaders how, where, and why you think the Lord is leading you. Ask them to pray with you about your direction. Seek their participation in your decision so they can have a shared sense of ownership in your plans as you move forward.

If after extended prayer you still believe God is directing you to missions but you have no sense of leading to a particular people, the Lord may want you to step out in faith.

---

6. Be encouraged, but also be faithful. God wants to reveal Himself and His heart to you in a very personal way. As you seek to draw closer to Him through intentional study, prayer, and listening, you will probably find yourself drawn to a particular people group.

7. Step out in faith. If after extended prayer you still believe God is directing you to missions but you have no sense of leading to a particular people, the Lord may want you to step out in faith. He may be asking you to move in obedience like Abraham—not certain where you're headed, but knowing that He will point the way.

Most sending agencies and sending churches are happy to walk with you during your process of searching for an assignment. They're interested in matching your gifts with the task to be done. They want to see you placed on a team where your abilities and gifts will complement the mix of the rest of the group.

You will probably be asked to take personality inventories and tests on things like vocational and role preferences, psychological background, conflict resolution style, and linguistic ability. While these exercises may seem like a lot of paperwork, they're not "busywork." All the information you gather will help you, your church, and the agency determine whether you're well suited to work with them. Research and experience have shown that for success in language learning, for example, motivation is as important as natural aptitude. Keep in mind, too, that these are tools for self-understanding and assessment, not final answers.

For further insights on choosing an agency, take a look at the following article and the Decision-Making Worksheet on page 78.

BIBLICAL "ROAD SIGNS" TO GUIDE YOUR DECISION-MAKING

Steve Hoke

Christian decision-making involves freedom and risk. Scripture teaches us to confirm God's moral will (as revealed in the Bible) by following certain indicators—I call them "wisdom signs." These signs are specific biblical ways the Holy Spirit guides us in our decision-making.

Types of Decisions

Christian decision-making can be divided into two categories. The first involves *areas that are specifically addressed in the Bible*. These are the revealed principles and commands of God, which must be obeyed. Those scriptural guidelines—both exhortations and prohibitions—shape our lifestyles as believers.

The second category involves *areas where the Bible gives no command or principle to follow*. In these situations, it's the believer's responsibility to freely choose his or her own course of action within the boundaries of biblical guidelines.

Now, how do these apply to the specific decisions we face—which church to attend, for example, or which career to pursue, or whether we're to marry and have children? Does God provide help for these life decisions beyond the general guidelines set forth in His Word?

We believe God is a personal and loving God—not a detached, aloof being. He invites us to know Him and tells us that He has counted the very hairs of our heads. Since He's so personally involved in our lives, how, then, do we understand His mind for us when we face a specific decision?

Scripture describes the following seven "wisdom signs." These indicators can help you discover and affirm the Lord's will for your life.

1. Common sense. God created people with a natural ability to make sound judgments based on facts. It's a form of wisdom that's part of God's grace to humans everywhere (Prov. 1:1-3; 3:5-6; 4:11).

When it comes to selecting a mission experience, common sense tells you to compare things like the mission organization's purpose, programs, leaders, supervision, fields, and costs. It causes you to look at your own abilities, experiences, and spiritual gifts.

> *When two options you are considering seem truly equal, this wisdom sign tells you to choose the one you would enjoy most—follow your heart!*

Common sense works as a "wisdom sign" as long as it harmonizes with the moral will of God and does not contradict what He has already revealed in Scripture.

2. Spiritual counsel. The book of Proverbs teaches that there is balance and wisdom in seeking the wise counsel of mature believers (Prov. 10:23; 15:22; 19:20; Heb. 13:7,8). These may include parents, close friends, teachers, pastors, or others in spiritual leadership. The Christian corrective to the extremes of individualism is the wisdom and support of the Christian community—the church—of which you are a member.

If the advice of certain counselors conflicts at points, evaluate the reasons behind their differing viewpoints. Keep in mind the strong points of each type of counselor: Your parents probably know you best; teachers and professional counselors can help you uncover conceptual blind spots you've overlooked; pastors and other spiritual counselors can put facts and situations into proper spiritual perspective.

3. Personal desires. Spiritual growth makes a significant impact on your personal desires. The psalmist wrote that when you delight in the Lord, He gives you "the desires of your heart" (Ps. 37:4; Prov. 19:21; 21:21).

As you mature, your motives and desires often reflect God's desires. But your personal desires are never authoritative and must always be judged against God's Word.

When two options you are considering seem truly equal, this wisdom sign tells you to choose the one you would enjoy most—follow your heart!

4. Circumstances. The situation and context in which you will find yourself become vital ingredients in decision-making.

Carefully analyze your situation (Prov. 16:9, 33; 20:24). As you contemplate missions involvement, your situation will include factors like time, people, cost, travel, and so on. Every option has its advantages and disadvantages. Try to discern the more subtle consequences of your decisions.

Writing down an idea can be an antidote to emotionalizing your decision or becoming a victim of your own impulsiveness. Rather than looking at your circumstances to detect some hidden clue from God, use the pieces of your reality to help you make decisions.

5. Scripture. God's moral will is objective, complete, and adequate as revealed in His Word. Yet the Bible does not tell us the precise answer to every situation. What it *does* tell us is to acquire wisdom and to apply it to our decisions (Prov. 6:20-23; 8:10-11, 32-33; 9:10).

We've all had ideas pop into our heads. Those inner impressions can come from a variety of sources—God, Satan, past experience, stress, the flesh, immaturity, indigestion, insomnia—and must be judged by God's Word. After thoughtful consideration, you may conclude that an impression or feeling is actually a good plan—a wise way to serve God. Or you may decide it's foolish and ought to be ignored.

6. Prayer. Prayer is your means of communicating with God to understand His mind and His guidance. In most decisions, this is where the battle is fought (Eph. 6:18).

The time you spend thinking and gathering information about a decision should be matched with daily conversations in prayer. At times it helps to focus these prayers by writing them down. I have known people who agonize over major decisions, but spend less than five minutes a day praying about them. If you are trusting God as your loving Father, doesn't it make sense that He is eager to answer your requests for wisdom through the intimate channel of prayer?

7. Previous experience. Life is a classroom, and you don't want to return to second grade if you can help it! Be smart. Reflect on your past decisions—and those of others—to learn how they were good for you and how they were bad (Prov. 10:24; 21:1). Write down any critical decisions that influence where you now are and what options you have before you.

Romans 8:28 says that God is at work in every decision you make as a Christian committed to His will. This means that when you make the best decision possible, you can trust Him to work out the results for good.

Let God's peace be the final confirmation that you have made a wise decision, and move out confidently in obedience.

A Worksheet

The Decision-Making Worksheet on page 78 can serve as a model of a "balance sheet" of the pros and cons for each specific decision you're facing.

It's a simple, logical tool to help guide your thinking and reflection. By referring to the seven wisdom signs listed in the left column of the worksheet, you are seeking to listen to each of the major areas of guidance mentioned in Scripture in your decision-making process. Meanwhile, don't forget that God has committed Himself to be at work in your deliberations for the ultimate purpose of His greater glory.

Personal Experience

When facing a major decision, I start a separate worksheet for each option I'm considering. I record the pros and cons as I carefully work through each wisdom sign. This may take days or sometimes weeks. Some may see this as

too mechanized or lacking spontaneity, yet that same person will take weeks evaluating what car or computer to purchase. So if it's important, I think it's worth the effort.

I find the process is a discipline that helps me be more prayerful and careful. It doesn't make it easier; it just makes the issues clearer. In every decision I've made since high school, it has clarified my need to wait on God. It doesn't replace dependence; rather, it makes painfully obvious the areas in which I really am totally dependent upon the Lord.

Use the worksheet as a spiritual decision-making aid; it's not a gimmick or a ouji board game. But if you've been confused by the number of options you face, and the details and issues seem to multiply, this tool is guaranteed to spotlight the wisdom factors you should consider.

As you take time to think and pray through what insight and wisdom you've gained from each wisdom sign, write down those insights in the appropriate column. When you've completed your "homework," prayerfully, you may find that the sheer weight of wisdom for one option very clearly outweighs the pros or cons of another option. And that's the purpose of the tool—to help you determine which option would be the wisest decision to make.

Peace. When the wisdom signs seem to point toward a particular choice, bathe your final decision in prayer. When you sense God's *peace* about that option, you can be pretty sure it's a wise decision (Col. 3:15). Let God's peace be the final confirmation that you have made a wise decision, and move out confidently in obedience.

Note: You may want to make copies of the worksheet to write on when you get ready to evaluate more than one option.

DECISION-MAKING WORKSHEET

Description of decision to be made:		

Date:		Deadline:	

WISDOM SIGNS	PROS	CONS
Common Sense		
Spiritual Counselors		
Personal Desires		
Circumstances		
Scripture		
Prayer		
Previous Decisions		
Peace		

JOURNAL WORKSHEET 6

WHERE ARE YOU NOW?

Do you know missionaries who are attempting to reach an unreached people? Who? Where? _____

_____

Is your church supporting missionaries or national workers who are reaching unreached peoples? _____

_____

Are you reasonably familiar with many different cultures and people groups from around the world? _____

_____

List the top three people groups which currently interest you.

1. _____

2. _____

3. _____

WHAT DO YOU NEED TO DO NEXT?

When will you discuss the needs of the world with your church or a mission agency? Which one? _____

_____

When and how will you do your own investigating on unreached people groups or other majorly unevangelized parts of the world with whom you might become involved? _____

_____

What continent? _____

What nation(s)/region? _____

Which people group(s)? _____

List at least three specific learning objectives you will set for yourself as you research unreached people(s):

1. _____

2. _____

3. _____

WHAT WILL THE FUTURE LOOK LIKE?

What *kind* of missionary do you believe God is leading you to become? (In other words, what will be your special niche within a church planting assignment?) _____

_____

Where do you believe He will have you serve? _____

_____

With what church or agency might you serve? _____

With what people group or geographic location will you be involved? _____

STEP 7: HANDS-ON MISSIONARY TRAINING

Steve Hoke

Let's assume you've completed your basic academic training. Let's also assume you've had serious on-the-job ministry training within a local church—and (hopefully) have been gainfully employed in the meantime!

Assuming all these things means that by now you have probably spent at least one brief period of time in another culture, and perhaps as long as two years in a ministry-focused local or international short-term or cross-cultural experience. You've been stretched. You've been shaken. And you've grown stronger as a result.

Now it's time to figure out what kind of practical missionary training and/or advanced training you're going to need. Our focus here is to highlight practical equipping for the particular kind of ministry work you will do on the field. We know of some church planters whose only stateside ministry experience was discipling high school students and teaching an adult Sunday school class. This is neither adequate nor realistic practical training for persons who will be ministering in multilevel, multicultural contexts.

By now you may have determined the kind of missionary role you want to fill. This workbook centers on leading you toward a role in church planting. But bivocational (tentmaking) ministry and training/mentoring other missionaries are examples of other vital roles toward which God may be directing you. As you know by now, we're assuming that all these roles contribute to the ultimate goal of taking the gospel to a group of people who have never heard it before and being used by the Holy Spirit to plant a community of Jesus worshipers in their midst. In other words, a missionary is one who is trying to reach less-reached or unreached people with the Good News of Christ. These unreached peoples are located all over the world. Some live in cities. Some are in suburban areas. Some are

in remote rural communities or tribes. Perhaps by now you know specifically that God is calling you to work with a remote tribal group or within one of the exploding "megacities." Maybe you know where you're going and the church or agency you'll partner with.

Perhaps God has shown you a particular continent, country, or people group among whom He wants you to minister. Maybe you've had the opportunity to study the many needs for a holistic ministry that have been identified there. You may feel led by the Spirit to attempt to reach a particular one. Or you may be part of a church with a particular missions focus, such as sending church based teams to plant churches among an "adopted" unreached people group or nation.

All these factors will affect the extent and type of practical missionary training you will need. It will require time and actual ministry experience to develop competencies in all three of the dimensions described in the profiles—character and spirituality qualities, ministry skills, and knowledge goals. You'll need to drive your foundations deep into the substrata of God Himself.

Master the fundamentals. First, you must build a solid God and Word foundation—a strong working knowledge of Scripture that establishes your faith, undergirds your values, and guides your behavior. Second, you must have a good grasp of the cultures within which the Scriptures were written. Without this, you will be unable to communicate God's Word effectively to another culture. Third, you will dream of the day when this living Word comes supernaturally alive in a new culture.

Your biblical knowledge is to be valued, not because it affords prestige or power, but because it is useful for guiding your ministry. It enables you to be and/or do what would otherwise be impossible. That's why, in the profile on pages 26-27, we focused first on character qualities ("being" goals) and ministry skills ("doing" goals). Those first two qualifications help you determine what knowledge you need to acquire for effective missionary service.

Build a solid set of ministry skills. If your work on the field is to be effective, your missionary training should be intentional and purposeful. Your early on-the-job training in a church was meant to expose you to the range of ministries needed in a church and to stretch your ministry "muscles" while letting you try your hand at teaching, witnessing, discipling, and so on. This practical training phase of your preparation is a time in which you need to sharpen the specific ministry skills you will most likely use overseas. Hopefully you were part of a church based cell group team that witnessed growth and even multiplied itself.

Knowing your role is critical to focusing your training. The most relevant preparation for church planting overseas is participation in and significant responsibility on a church planting team *at home*. Witnessing in your neighborhood, door-to-door canvassing, starting evangelistic Bible studies, creating cell groups, raising up leaders from the harvest, and discipling new believers to the second and third generation are critical church planting skills. These are practical traits you can acquire, develop, and refine in your own congregation.

You must have adequate missiological and theological preparation, including an understanding of God's purposes in history, how His Spirit has worked in the history of the church, how theology has developed, and the way men and women through the ages have worked out their understanding of what God has been saying to us. But keep it practical. The purpose of this study is to help you be more effective in living and equipping others to live meaningful, Christ-centered lives. *Your knowledge is never an end in itself.*

Avoid simplistic mission slogans and sloppy reductionism of the Great Commission. Develop a strong theology of creation and of kingdom values. Many missionaries have greatly benefited from one to three years of formal studies, but it doesn't work that way for others.

The "Perspectives on the World Christian Movement" course is the single best introduction to a theology of international missions. If you haven't yet taken the course, now is the time to do so. See Appendix 2 for details on how to enroll.

You must have broad training in the social sciences, especially anthropology, sociology, and political science. These disciplines go hand in hand with the history and present effectiveness of missionary work around the world.

Anthropology enables you to consider the origin and nature of cultures—your own and that of the people you will be serving. Sociology provides a vocabulary and mental models for understanding how people establish rules for living together. Political science gives you tools for understanding the dynamic tensions that flow (or rip) through societies and how societies organize themselves politically. As missionaries learn about the beliefs and customs of a people, they discover effective bridges for the communication of biblical truth.

Language and culture learning are of supreme importance. No effort should be spared here. Wise churches and most sending agencies have a clear policy that lays out the orientation, cultural study, and language proficiency expected of all missionaries. However, because this can be one of the most difficult parts of practical missionary training, some churches and agencies may ease off the requirements in this area.

> Language and culture learning are of supreme importance. No effort should be spared here. Churches and mission agencies should encourage missionaries to do more than the required minimum.

Actually, churches and mission agencies should encourage missionaries to do *more* than the required minimum. There are hundreds of missionaries who would say with regret, "How I wish that years ago we had spent the time and the effort to become fluent in the language! The demands of family, the needs of the field, and the 'tyranny of the urgent' drew us into ministry with less than adequate adult literacy. As a result, the impact of our ministry was lessened over the course of our missionary career. Don't repeat our experience!"

Language acquisition and culture learning go hand in hand. It's difficult to really understand a culture until you can *think* in its terms—until you can use its idioms, laugh at its jokes, weep at its pain. Thinking culturally requires fluency in the language, and not just the trade language used in the cities, either.

Missionaries desperately need to speak the heart language or dialect of the local people in their communities and villages. As a friend of ours says, "You want to communicate fluently in the language that people think in, dream in, and make love in!"

Most North Americans have little training in language learning and language theory. The majority of us are monolingual. The rest of the world is not. That puts us at a disadvantage when it comes to learning a language. Therefore, a basic understanding of language theory or linguistics may prove useful before you plunge into learning a new language. In addition, it's even more useful to study some of the new language acquisition techniques that have recently been developed.

> *Don't let a negative experience of trying to learn a language in high school prejudice you. Your classroom attempts may not have been a true test of your abilities at all!*

One of the most effective language acquisition methods is to learn among people who speak the language. Tom and Betty Sue Brewster pioneered the LAMP (Language Acquisition Made Practical) method in the 1970s. The method emphasizes learning simple phrases and repeatedly using them while living with a host family or conversing regularly with a local "language helper" from your target culture. This "total immersion" approach to learning language and culture is the most natural way of "bonding" with your new culture. Today it is widely practiced by many mission agencies as a primary language acquisition technique.

As the world becomes more urban, there's a growing emphasis on preparing missionaries to live and minister in cities. Missions internships in urban centers throughout North America provide ideal preparation for incarnational living among city dwellers, especially the urban poor.

For instance, each summer several mission agencies and local churches jointly sponsor an eight- to 10-week urban internship in Los Angeles. Missionary appointees learn while ministering in a context similar to that of the "target people" to whom they'll eventually go. Each participant lives with a family from the ethnic group with whom he or she plans to minister. Faculty come from participating churches, mission agencies, and nearby seminaries. The participants' training includes highly interactive on-site cultural exposure and investigation, LAMP methods of language acquisition, spiritual formation (including biblical study and reflection), team building, and leadership development. Similar training programs are conducted by other agencies and churches in other major cities such as New York and Chicago. (For further specifics, see the Missions Training Directory in Appendix 3.)

Several other innovative language study programs, like that of the Russian Language Ministry at Columbia International University in Columbia, South Carolina, have arisen in response to the growing demand of North Americans who are moving to Eastern Europe and regions of unreached peoples. Based on recent developments in linguistics and language learning, these U.S. based programs provide a solid foundation in language basics within a stable, more familiar environment before you move overseas and encounter cultural and language stress. Thankfully, there are two-week intensive courses that provide language learning skills for you. Check these options out.

Don't fall into the trap of thinking you will only have to learn one language in your lifetime. God may move you to another field. The future of missions will see an increasing redeployment of missionaries from one country to another, often in mid-career.

Having an ability to learn other languages increases your flexibility, making you ready to take new assignments elsewhere in the kingdom. And don't let a negative experience of trying to learn a language in high school prejudice you. Your classroom attempts may not have been a true test of your abilities at all!

If North Americans are weak in speaking other languages, they are even weaker in understanding and being sensitive to other cultures. North America is such a large continent, and one can travel such vast distances without encountering large groups of people who are "not like us" that, at least until recently, we have had very little understanding and appreciation of other cultures. Despite the cultural diversity that has enriched North American culture for over 200 years, we have tended to see it as a rather bland "melting pot" of many cultures rather than a "stew pot" or "tossed salad" of coexisting, rather distinctive cultures and peoples. Certainly the '90s have brought us a new emphasis on diversity and inclusiveness, and Generation X has a broader perspective on culture and the world than did most of our ancestors. Yet the headlines frequently testify to the fact that North Americans still tend to *react* to differences, rather than accepting and celebrating them. Thankfully, this situation is radically changing as the "nations" flow again into North America.

The history of missions includes countless examples of sincere but sad attempts to reach a people—attempts made by missionaries who understood neither their own culture nor the culture of the people they were trying to reach. Learning about the culture right next door to you will start you on the path toward learning to be a "cultural detective"—naturally inquisitive and genuinely interested in learning about other people and comprehending their ways of life.

The first step is to understand yourself and your own cultural background and biases.

For resources on schools and other sources of practical missionary training, including language and culture learning, check out the directory in Appendix 3.

WHY OVERSEAS MISSIONARY TRAINING WORKS

Swimming Is Best Learned Wet

Roger Charles

Rice paddies surrounded the seminary where Dirk studied church planting. Friends debated the theory and practice of Muslim evangelism over heaping bowls of rice and chili peppers. The competing melodies of Indonesian church music and the call to prayer at a dozen nearby mosques set the mood for his theological studies. Crowded dorms and buses and the lack of clocks and electricity taught Dirk volumes about the values and realities of ministry in another culture. The farmers in his village church grew to respect the foreigner who was first a learner, then a teacher.

After graduating from the Indonesian seminary, Dirk wrote, "I have found that my impact on Asians is largely measured by Asia's impact on me. Overseas training has brought me thousands of miles closer to the hearts of those I want to serve. I believe this extra cultural learning has added an incarnational freshness to my ministry that rings true with the lifestyle of Jesus and the apostles."

Taking the Plunge

Dirk and many other aspiring missionaries have experienced the strengths and weaknesses of overseas training. Many came from strong local churches and top Bible schools, yet they recognized gaps in their cross-cultural preparation. Overseas training provided the right tools for their job and exposed them to real cross-cultural living. Though they went about it in different ways, cultural immersion was their common goal.

Missionaries often mistake plunging into ministry for plunging into culture. They pay for a fast trip through language school by enduring years of slow and pain-filled ministry. Some are disillusioned and discouraged when what were great ministry skills and experience in the U.S. are not immediately useful overseas.

> *Missionaries often mistake plunging into ministry for plunging into culture. They pay for a fast trip through language school by enduring years of slow and pain-filled ministry.*

Swimming is best learned wet. Before missionaries face the pounding surf of full-time ministry, they need a chance to paddle around, flounder, and right themselves in shallower waters. The mistakes that knock them down need time to be transformed from failure to insight.

Slowing down at the beginning for a mixture of formal and informal on-site training can immensely accelerate their ensuing climb up the learning curve to high-quality ministry.

Seminary Overseas

Dirk's seminary classes were all taught in the Indonesian language. He planted and pastored a church on weekends. He interned on a local missionary team. Academically, he could have done better in America. But his experience has made him a cultural insider with a large network of Indonesian pastors and leaders. He's now teaching and writing training materials with a distinctly Asian focus and flavor.

Of course, full-time theological training is not for everyone, even when linked with plenty of hands-on ministry. Australians Barry and Mary entered the same seminary program as Dirk, but unlike him they did not have a mission board to shepherd them. The Indonesian school's time demands were overwhelming and not geared for a foreign family. Barry and Mary decided to slow down and study part-time. That helped.

After a year of language and a year of part-time studies, Barry and Mary found their ministry niche on a team targeting a large unreached people group. Now they can start this focused ministry having already overcome many family and cultural problems.

Seminary anywhere is difficult. In another language it is often incomprehensible. For those interested in a year or two of study near but not immersed in a foreign culture, seminary programs in English are available in the Philippines, Singapore, India, and several African and Latin American countries.

Wading in Gradually

Sharon was headed for Thailand. She received one month of candidate orientation in the U.S., then three months of training in Singapore. There she was directly exposed to Asian cultural issues. She studied culture and missions with full-time missionaries. She learned to eat hot sauce on rice by adding one drop each day. Her entry into the culture and language of Thailand, which is so radically different from the U.S., was moderated by a general introduction and immersion into Asia.

Sharon's cultural training was just beginning when she went from Singapore to Thailand for 12 months of language school. Then, for her first term, her mission gave her a culturally intense assignment and evaluated her language progress quarterly.

Sharon spent that first two-year term living in a Christian girls' hostel, surrounded by Thai friends, Thai food, and the Thai language. After leading Bible studies and worship for hundreds of evenings over those two years, Sharon's degree of language fluency and cultural adaptation astonished her family, friends, and even other missionaries.

Building on Short Terms

Overseas training is the logical extension of "see it first" ministry visits. Cultural immersion provides purposeful mastery of the cultural adaptation skills necessary for an interested visitor to become an effective resident.

Amy took this route. She had gone on several short-term trips to the Philippines. Those experiences whetted her appetite for missions and gave her a desire to return as a long-term missionary.

> *Overseas training is the logical extension of "see it first" ministry visits. Cultural immersion provides purposeful mastery of the cultural adaptation skills necessary for an interested visitor to become an effective resident.*

She enrolled in the Asian studies program at the University of the Philippines. For two years she studied in the city and ministered in a church in the countryside.

Amy wrote a thesis on traditional Filipino healing and spiritism, gaining a much deeper understanding of these crucial spiritual issues than do most of the busy long-term missionaries. At her graduation awards banquet, following several dull speeches in English by Filipinos, Amy gave a glowing speech with a Christian message in clear, formal Tagalog. She received thundering applause.

Cultural immersion had turned a bold short-term visitor into a powerful cross-cultural communicator.

Cultural Apprenticeship

Dave and Eve had been on short-term mission trips before their local church sent them to Hong Kong as full-time missionaries. Their assignment was to assist a Chinese friend who was researching the church in mainland China.

While studying Mandarin, Dave began writing a prayer guide on the Chinese church. His cultural and political understanding grew rapidly. Without shepherding and supervision, however, his family was nearing burnout.

Dave linked up with an effective field team and found the right balance of cultural apprenticeship with Chinese friends and ministry apprenticeships with American missionaries. Thereafter, his ministry to China and his web of relation-ships grew rapidly. Their "let's be learners first" attitude propelled Dave and Eve into a strategic program, which trains overseas Chinese to minister in mainland China.

Jack, on the other hand, leaped right into an intense international apprenticeship. He was a former Marine, but boot camp never prepared him for the challenges of ministry in inner-city Manila. So after a few months in a language immersion program, Jack joined an inner-city ministry to the poorest of Manila's street people. He lived with a band of Filipino street evangelists. The 20 of them slept in a room with narrow bunk beds crammed only 18 inches apart.

Jack ate, bathed, and slept "ghetto Christianity." He followed a Filipino leader everywhere for the first months, then was increasingly sent out to minister on his own. This was cultural boot camp in its most intense form. But in his two years on the streets, Jack won more souls than many lifelong missionaries in Manila and was frequently told by Filipinos, "You speak Tagalog better than we do!"

Seasoned Missionaries Too

Veteran missionaries can also benefit from overseas training opportunities. Rory, after losing his visa as a religious worker in a Muslim country, fulfilled a long-time dream by re-

entering the same country as a student. He learned a new regional language and had a chance to study the culture more deeply than when he'd been a busy church planting missionary. Also, he was able to maintain old relationships with his disciples and to informally mentor new missionaries who came to "his" country as tentmakers.

Ray, a senior mission agency administrator, decided to complete a doctorate in management in the Philippines rather than in the U.S. because the school there had a program in English and the location would enable him to spend time with his children, who were in an academy in Manila.

Ray spent one school quarter each year in the Philippines and maintained his ministry and administrative roles in another country the rest of the year. One product of his studies was the creation of an on-the-job training program for new field leadership within his agency. The agency had run similar programs in the U.S., but they were much more expensive to maintain. Ray's experience gave his agency the expertise needed to plan a new, less costly approach, while providing him with a valuable advanced degree.

Finding Overseas Programs

The cost of overseas missionary training is often quite low—especially compared to the high cost of seminary and the higher cost of first-term burnout! However, finding a well-rounded program that will stretch you without breaking you may take some time.

Christian international students and missionaries from your country of interest can provide insight on the missions training options available in their homeland. Missions professors and missions agency leaders are often also aware of good programs and the costs involved.

Variety is essential to missionary life and training. The best training experiences include most of the following personal spiritual preparation: language learning from people, not books; living with nationals; some structured goals and activities; a national and a foreign mentor; occasional fellowship and spiritual support with missionaries; adequate rest and recreation; a supportive home church and mission committee.

The spiritual food served up by missionaries who train overseas will taste a lot more like home cooking to the people they serve.

Just as some people can handle spicier food than others, some potential missionaries are able to handle more aggressive training programs. But don't overestimate your capabilities. Generally, you should settle for a balanced diet of training with a distinctly foreign flavor. The spiritual food served up by missionaries who train overseas will taste a lot more like home cooking to the people they serve.

Roger Charles (a pseudonym) has participated in cultural immersion programs in several countries. He currently trains Asians in cross-cultural communications, comparative religions, and New Testament theology.

Reprinted from Mission Today '96 with permission of the publisher. Evanston, IL: Berry Publishing, 1996.

CUSTOMIZE YOUR MISSION TRAINING

Steve Hoke

There's a world of learning beyond the classroom. It's practical. It's guided. It's culturally specific. And it's offered by some of the finest agencies in the world. More and more, mission agencies are designing their own customized training for the specific fields and people groups they serve. These in-house programs will teach you principles and skills that are best learned on the job. The instruction begins at home, intensifies on the mission field, and covers the following 10 critical dimensions:

Pre-Field Training: Before Going to the Field

1. Ministry philosophy. The core values and beliefs that guide every missionary effort are better "caught" than taught—best learned by rubbing shoulders with missionaries and national coworkers. The conceptual foundation for a mission's philosophy is presented in a pre-field orientation or candidate school that lasts from one week to three months. You'll see it at work when you get to the field. Principles from Scripture, research, and field experience are shared to help you develop spiritual, cross-cultural, and relational skills.

One mission executive says, "Our four-month pre-field training program is the single most important factor in preventing field casualties." Yet hearing about an agency's philosophy while sitting in Denver is one thing; learning it in incarnational ministry in Calcutta is the real thing. No matter what the ministry, new missionaries develop their own personalized philosophy of ministry best in the cross-cultural crucible. Another exec explains: "We are looking for team players, but we fully expect to help new staff learn how we disciple, build, and plant new churches.... Once we find a strong player, we're committed to making them even more effective through teamwork."

2. Message. Each mission crafts and channels the gospel message in creative ways that reflect its own style of ministry. Campus Crusade, Navigators, and InterVarsity are just three groups that have helped two generations of young people share their faith through distinctively clear and concise presentations. Initial workshops familiarize you with the basic presentation style of an agency, while on-the-job training and practice in the "seminary of the streets" expand your understanding and hone your skills.

There are also rich messages in a mission's "hidden curriculum," which is comprised of the values, beliefs, lifestyle, language, and culture they have developed over the years. Spontaneous expression of an ongoing gratitude to God for His grace and His goodness is the "life message" characteristic of one particular mission. A mission's "message" will rub off on you as you work alongside them.

3. Money. Some of the finest coaching input you can receive on stewardship of time, talent, and treasure comes from mission training programs. The essentials of trusting God for every detail of life—living by faith—form the bedrock of missionary support raising and are taught by veterans who empathize with you in this faith-building process. Skills in budgeting and handling money are developed under experienced tutors. The basics of both "friend raising" and fund raising are mastered under caring mentors who walk with you through the process.

4. Meaning. The shape, color, and flavor of a message influences the meaning it conveys. Mission agencies help you comprehend the implications of Jesus' message both for your own life and the lives of new disciples. In-service training can foster greater spiritual effectiveness and power in your own life. This, in turn, invests

---

Increasingly, missions have specialized target peoples which demand customized strategies. Focused outreach to Muslims, Chinese, migrant workers, Hindus, Buddhists, or animists requires intensive, specialized, on-field training by skilled national and missionary practitioners.

---

your communication with renewed vigor and meaning for others. Each mission's distinctive programs add layers of meaning to Christian ministry which are unique to their approach. What were formerly only clichés or concepts soon become life-changing truths. You're introduced to new ideas before you go, but you'll only find nourishment in these truths when you digest them for yourself in the heat of battle.

5. Methods. Mission agencies teach fresh and different ways to communicate the Good News across language and cultural barriers. Ministry methods vary from personal evangelism and discipleship programs to specialized linguistic and anthropological training. Missions typically teach the use of ministry skills and specialized materials during on-field internships that last from one month to two years. They involve informal meetings and interviews, formal classes, and scheduled practicum in areas such as lifestyle evangelism, discipling others, urban church planting, street preaching, or leader training.

Increasingly, missions have specialized target peoples which demand customized strategies. Focused outreach to Muslims, Chinese, migrant workers, Hindus, Buddhists, or animists requires intensive, specialized, on-field training by skilled national and missionary practitioners. Language learning is best done on-site as well and can last from two months to two years before fluency is developed.

6. Models of ministry. Each mission has developed a design or pattern for the way it does ministry, whether evangelism, discipleship, or church planting. This becomes a framework around which ministry is planned. Many missions intentionally teach the principles that undergird their approach to ministry. Approaches vary from street theater and preaching to cell group evangelism in high-rise communities, from research based church planting to literature distribution or university evangelism. An agency's model of ministry can enhance your own emerging view of cross-cultural mission and stretch you into more creative means of reaching people for Christ. You should observe critically and listen carefully—trying to detect the pattern of coworkers, willing to adapt your own ideas of how missions should be conducted.

7. Models and mentors. Every mission has its share of gentle giants. They may be the formal leaders or the informal, unobtrusive leaders who influence an entire movement. Time alone with them is a powerful training experience—life-on-life exposure to God's "Hall of Famers." They aren't flawless, but they know how to play the game!

If you really want to distill the experience people like this carry, you may need to seek them out and ask for time alone with them. If you can, design an internship or apprenticeship under the guidance and mentoring of a veteran missionary or national pastor whose character and life you respect and whose ministry you want to emulate. Don't be afraid to ask, "Will you mentor me?"

8. Management style. Within days of joining a mission agency, you'll begin to pick up pointers and principles of managing ministry and working with people. Take advantage of opportunities to learn lessons on faith, courage, planning, organizing, leading, imparting vision, budgeting, coaching, and evaluating ministry from godly men and women.

Every mission agency has a distinctive style of management. Some are very Western in their approach, setting measurable objectives and evaluating progress. Others are much more relaxed in how they recruit, train, and guide the flow of ministry. Some exert considerable control over lifestyle and ministry. Others allow more freedom and responsibility. Some are rigid, others flexible. Try to discern which management style fits you best. Learn all you can ahead of time about the dynamics and "chemistry" that make these teams work.

A pre-field orientation is helpful, but it is inadequate training for lifelong effectiveness. The initial training must be followed with specialized equipping on the field and supplemented with study breaks and ongoing educational opportunities on furloughs.

---

9. Maintenance. More and more mission agencies are realizing the importance of providing balanced "TLC" for their missionaries. This includes *training* and *lifelong* opportunities for *learning*, as well as *care* of missionaries and their families. A pre-field orientation is helpful, but it is inadequate training for lifelong effectiveness. The initial training must be followed with specialized equipping on the field and supplemented with study breaks and ongoing educational opportunities on furloughs.

Some missions have significant infrastructure and staff to serve missionary needs; others are quite lean and can offer little care. Some offer mid-career assessment and career counseling; others can only listen, encourage, and refer you to skilled professionals. Some agencies are developing reentry workshops to help returning missionaries decompress from the pressures of cross-cultural living. These workshops involve reflecting on their experience in groups with other missionaries and talking about their expectations of what lies ahead. The key to healthy reentry is knowing how to maintain your spiritual, relational, and physical strength despite a radically different schedule and setting.

Agencies are also increasingly concerned with missionary care and nurture, with helping their missionaries develop personal maintenance programs that keep them plugged in and turned on. Caring for the education, transitions, and well-being of missionary kids is a significant ministry of larger organizations. Counseling services, career assessments, and retirement planning are areas that round out a mission's care program.

10. Mobilization. Mission agencies can also teach you to be more effective in mobilizing others for missions. Your experience can be a great magnet for others, convincing them of the need to become World Christians. You can allow your own experience of cross-cultural ministry to serve as a powerful model. A mission agency can help you be on the lookout for those who will respond to the burden of your heart for missions and who will share in the challenge to pray, give, and serve.

After your formal training, you can look forward to discovering a unique world of learning. It's personal. It's powerful. It's life-changing. Be prepared to meet some of the finest teachers and godly mentors in God's academy. Unlike formal programs burdened with requirements and financial costs, mission agencies provide personalized training—custom fit to your gifts and background. These non-formal programs will give you hands-on expertise in face-to-face ministry that has direct impact on peoples' lives, teaching you skills that are best learned on the job. The instruction you've already received has only just begun. It keeps getting better. And so will you.

Reprinted from *Missions Today '96* with permission of the publisher. Evanston, IL: Berry Publishing, 1996.

JOURNAL WORKSHEET 7

WHERE ARE YOU NOW?

What information do you have now about churches, schools, and other sources of practical missionary training? _____

_____

_____

_____

What information do you have about graduate schools or advanced training in culture and language? _____

_____

_____

_____

What other languages can you read or speak? Have you ever studied another language? How did it go? _____

_____

_____

_____

Have you ever been in a situation that required you to understand a culture quite different from your own? How did you learn about the culture? How well did you adapt to it? _____

_____

_____

_____

Whom do you know that may be able to counsel you on practical training and/or graduate schools?

- Pastors: _____
- Missionaries: _____
- Christian staff on campus: _____
- Friends at church: _____

WHAT DO YOU NEED TO DO NEXT?

Talk with your church leaders about practical training programs and look through the resources in the appendices. Then, list three training programs or graduate schools you're interested in attending.

1. _____

2. _____

3. _____

When will you discuss ways and means of learning language with your church, school counselors, and mission agency?

_____

_____

_____

When and how will you work out an integrated program of language and culture learning? _____

_____

_____

_____

Which school(s) will you visit, call, e-mail, or write? When? _____

_____

_____

_____

WHAT WILL THE FUTURE LOOK LIKE?

With some understanding of your financial situation, how much time should you plan to set aside for practical training and/or graduate school? _____

_____

_____

What language school or program might you attend for language acquisition in this country? List your options. Then rank them by considering quality, location, scheduling, and tuition.

1. _____

2. _____

3. _____

What specific languages will you need to know to reach the people to whom you feel God is leading you? _____

_____

_____

How would gaining some actual on-the-job field experience reshape your training plans? _____

_____

_____

_____

Would it be best for you to "sandwich" your graduate school training within a meaty layer of field experience? _____

_____

_____

_____

How does all this relate to your marriage and/or family plans? _____

_____

_____

_____

_____

_____

_____

_____

Phase 3:
Getting Established – Bonding

Step 8: Apprenticeships and Internships

Step 9: Lifelong Learning

Step 10: Finishing Strong

STEP 8:
APPRENTICESHIPS AND INTERNSHIPS

Steve Hoke

A field internship (sometimes called a "new staff" position) is an opportunity to develop understanding in your hosts' language and culture. It generally entails no other ministry responsibilities; your only job is to become proficient in the language and culture. Hopefully, a qualified and experienced missionary or national leader will then work with you to build your ministry on what his or her experience can teach.

If you're still in college, being an apprentice or an intern in cross-cultural service may seem years away. It probably is. But one way to prepare for the future is to understand it better. While we can't forecast exactly what the future holds, we *can* make plans and decisions that affect it.

Your expectations will significantly shape the nature of your experience. When you take a new job, it seldom turns out to be all you expected it would be. New experiences are like that. The same will be true of your first cross-cultural assignment. That doesn't mean you should expect to be "bummed out." But you should, by faith, hold your initial expectations loosely. Bring them before the Lord with open hands, willing to let Him shape or replace them.

Missions is going to be tougher than you imagine, but hang in there. It's worth it!

Your cross-cultural experience will stretch you and deepen you. Be ready for the most intense period of personal, family, and ministry growth in your life. The spiritual battle will stretch you and build your spiritual muscles. Living in community with an international team of Christians will feel like a crucible experience—being crushed under pressure and remolded amid heat. Anticipating that experience with realistic faith will increase your dependence upon the Lord and your commitment to being a vital member of your ministry community. And if you are married (with or without children), prepare for added stresses and challenges.

> *Be ready for the most intense period of personal, family, and ministry growth in your life. The spiritual battle will stretch you and build your spiritual muscles.*

There is much you can do to understand what it will be like. Ask your church and mission agency questions that will help you prepare.

A template for a first-year internship experience is described below. It's followed by a description of one couple's actual internship in Caracas, Venezuela. As you read these samples, seriously consider how you can adapt the model to your own situation in order to maximize your first year on the field.

MODEL FOR A FIRST-YEAR ON-FIELD INTERNSHIP
Steve Hoke

The following outline of an actual training model describes the procedure, assumptions, and activities that could guide your first year on the field. It is meant to give you a clear idea of the expectations, opportunities, and resources available. This model may be adapted by your church or agency.

Assumptions

1. You have completed both a pre-field orientation workshop and language acquisition workshop before going overseas. This training has given you an overview of the requisite attitudes, sensitivities, and skills for culture learning.

2. You have gained some advance exposure to your new language through Berlitz, LAMP, or an equivalent intensive language learning program.

3. Beyond the general pre-field orientation to cross-cultural living and communicating, the best place to learn culture-specific information and language is in the host culture. "Bonding" with the local people and their culture is critical to your long-term success in feeling at home in your new culture. (See Tom and Betty Sue Brewster's book *LAMP* for practical steps to bonding with your host culture.)

4. Language learning *is* ministry; hence, a deep commitment to gaining language proficiency as soon as possible (up to two years of full-time study), while continuing to bond and build relationships with host nationals, is necessary.

"Bonding" with the local people and their culture is critical to your long-term success in feeling at home in your new culture.

---

5. New missionaries should be exposed to as little non-preparatory ministry experience as is reasonable (i.e., without taking time away from the priority of language study).

6. A guided internship during your first year of language and culture learning is more effective and desirable than a completely spontaneous and unguided experience. You should have a mentor/coach to facilitate your entry, language learning, and general acculturation.

Learning Objectives

Upon completion of your first (or second, depending on the language) year in your expected location, you should be able to:

1. Carry on a simple conversation about spiritual matters (at an entry level) with a national, with 80% accuracy and comprehension.

2. Explain the history of the city and culture in which you live, highlighting key persons and events which have significantly influenced them.

3. Evidence a respect, sensitivity, and appreciation for the local culture, including its history, cultural values, food, and lifestyle.

Procedure

The following activities describe the type of learning activities that can be customized into a one-year internship experience:

• Consistently attend language classes and/or meet regularly with your language tutor.

• "Bond" with a local family by living with a host family for three weeks during your first six months on the field.

• Find and develop a relationship with a reliable cultural "informant" and model (if different from your tutor or host family).

• Develop a close relationship with a national family or couple, and vacation with them.

• Attend a national church with services in the national language.

• Participate in a national-led small group or cell group.

• Attend a church camp or retreat.

• Attend the national church's version of leadership training.

• Attend and observe at least three national cultural or religious festivals and celebrations.

• Visit three to six other national churches, across denominational lines.

• Conduct a personal prayer walk in your host city, and join others in other cities if possible.

• Complete the reading and study of the *Country Briefing Notebook and Reading Program* for "your" country.

• Visit at least two other cities and areas of interest in the country, with an eye toward observing regional distinctives, differences, and similarities, and toward learning about national history and culture.

• Keep a personal journal for the first 12 months, making entries at least weekly. Use your journal to guide intentional, critical reflection on your spiritual formation and culture learning.

Compare this general model with the following first-year itinerary of a real-life missionary couple in Caracas, Venezuela.

"BAREFOOTING": YOUR FIRST YEAR IN THE FIELD

Steve Hoke

First Six Months

Your **first three months** in Caracas are to be spent doing nothing but getting settled into a national home or your own place and adjusting to your new culture.

During this time you will:

1. Find housing and furnishings.
2. Meet your neighbors.
3. Immerse yourself in Spanish study (classroom, tutor, relationships).
4. Learn where to change money.
5. Learn how to get around using buses, taxis, and the subway.
6. Learn where the post office and stores are located.
7. Visit several different churches and ministries.
8. Learn how to use the phone, pay bills, pay rent, etc.
9. Find a Venezuelan mentor/helper (or "adopt" a family).
10. Obtain your *cedula* (official ID document), health certificates, and driver's licenses.

During your **second three months**, you will add to your adaptation skills by doing things like:

- Opening a bank account.
- Purchasing a car. (Note: Some may want to wait longer on this.)
- Finding a church home.

Second Six Months

Explore ministry possibilities.

1. Read the following:
   - Daily newspaper.
   - Weekly magazine.
   - A recent book that evaluates Venezuelan culture.

2. Visit and become acquainted with various resources and ministries in the city, including the following:
   - Christian bookstores.
   - The Caracas Ministerial (local pastors ministerial association).
   - The Evangelical Alliance.
   - Theological education centers.

3. Continue relationship building in your new church home.

Third Six Months

Begin structured ministry.

Expand your cultural understanding by attending/visiting the following:

- A wedding.
- A horse race.
- The theater.
- A funeral.
- A baseball game.
- The beach.
- A *barrio* (only after checking with your director regarding safety precautions).

Your ministry should gradually become more clearly defined. You will have a clearer picture of *what* you will do, *where*, *with whom*, and what *skills* you will need to do it.

Fourth Six Months

Focus on ministry development.

Some cautions:

- Watch the time you spend exclusively with people of your own nationality or ethnicity.
- Limit your time on e-mail. Already we have seen new missionaries misuse their time by e-mail. Give your cyberspace correspondent (even family) time to ponder the different exchange.
- Don't let other technology neutralize personal relationships.

JOURNAL WORKSHEET 8

WHERE ARE YOU NOW?

How does your church or mission agency prepare new missionaries for field service? _____

_____

Describe your picture of a good internship so you can compare it with what churches and agencies are actually doing.

_____

_____

WHAT DO YOU NEED TO DO NEXT?

Here are some questions to ask a church or mission agency about its first-year training program:

1. By the time I arrive on the field, how much orientation will I have received? _____

2. Where and when will my language learning take place? _____

3. What responsibilities will I have while I'm studying the language? _____

   _____

4. How long will all this take? _____

5. Where will I be assigned after language learning? _____

6. Will a missionary mentor/coach work with me? How? _____

   _____

7. How can I participate in the life of the national church *and* mission agency while on the field? _____

   _____

8. What first-term traps or barriers should I seek to avoid? _____

   _____

9. What competencies should I be building right now? _____

   _____

WHAT WILL THE FUTURE LOOK LIKE?

What internship programs exist related to the ministry location you're seeking? _____

_____

_____

What professional or mission associations should you relate to or join? What journals should you receive and read?

_____

_____

How can you keep abreast of developments and changes in missions as well as related to the country where you may live? _____

_____

_____

STEP 9: LIFELONG LEARNING

Steve Hoke

Caution: For those of you who are young adults, some of the following material may not appear to be highly relevant to you right now. Those of you who are older can rapidly discern the relevance of the following reflection exercise. Regardless of your age and experience, spend some time here. If you are younger, ask a mentor to work with you through the reflection. This may stimulate your mentor to think seriously. Another thing to keep in mind is that these exercises might best be done in small groups.

- A missionary of 20 years finds herself asking, "Which way next?"
- A mission leader realizes he is merely reacting to the demands of ministry. He has no focus and has lost sight of his unique giftedness and calling.
- The wife of a missionary has always sat in the shadows. She has significant capacity to minister, but no one has helped her clarify her ministry. Yet she has consistently devoted her efforts to helping and caring for others.

> *We will need to revise our concept of what a "term of service" means. The future of missions will probably bring much more mobility to our missionaries.*

These are all-too-familiar scenarios of missionaries who lack a perspective on their past and a focus on their future. And probably it's not their fault completely.

We will need to revise our concept of what a "term of service" means. The future of missions will probably bring much more mobility to our missionaries. Job contexts will change, or tasks will be completed, or more visas will be denied, or children will need special secondary education opportunities. Your cross-cultural skills may be used even in different countries or regions of the world. And as your gift mix and skill set mature, God will open up new and creative areas for you to grow as a person as well as in ministry.

How can you keep learning and growing?
- Read widely.
- Use home assignment (furlough) for specific courses or further degree programs.
- Take a study leave, take advantage of distance learning, or get into programs on the Internet.

The task of learning never ends. One challenging aspect of missionary life is that situations will always be new. There will always be fresh opportunities to learn and do new things. Your *perspective* on ongoing personal and professional development will be critical to your long-term effectiveness. Continuing to learn and grow as you minister will keep you fresh and on the cutting edge.

Getting sidetracked by the "tyranny of the urgent" and getting stressed out over trying to do too many tasks in too little time are just two of the typical traps encountered by the busy missionary who neglects his or her personal development. All too often, what's missing is a broader, longer-range perspective on what is important.

Robert Clinton has correctly observed, "The difference between leaders and followers is perspective. The difference between leaders and effectiveness is better perspective." More than ever before, missionaries recognize that leadership is demanding and difficult. If missionaries are to finish well in life and ministry, they will need all the perspective they can get.

The development of a mature Christian leader takes a lifetime. God refines our character, values, and leadership skills over a lifetime. A leader's development is the function of many events, people, and circumstances— "process items"—that leave an imprint on our lives and priorities. These milestones teach us significant life and ministry lessons.

Reflecting on God's ongoing work in our lives teaches us to recognize His activity. All leaders can point to critical incidents in which God taught them important insights that shaped their development.

Personal timeline. Your responses to God's shaping can be tracked on a timeline which helps evaluate your development, reveals your unique processing patterns, and provides a lifetime perspective. The exercise will help you chronicle how God has directed your life and shaped your identity.

You can gain insight for future ministry direction and decisions by comparing your development with the generalized development patterns of other Christian leaders or missionaries. This insight is part of what contributes to gaining a godly perspective.

Ministry ultimately flows out of being. Take time to create your personal timeline, and you'll accomplish an invaluable step toward gaining perspective and direction for the rest of your life. That's why we've included the Symbol Timeline Exercise below.

Over a lifetime, God shapes who we are. The main way He does this is through our life experience along the journey of faith. Because of this, setting aside intentional time for personal growth and development should be a vital component of every missionary's ministry plan.

We have tried to make it clear that we don't assume that all the preparation and training you need will be academic. Much of it will depend on the personal and professional growth goals you set for yourself.

With this in mind, a second way to be intentional in your lifelong development is to set goals for personal growth.

The **Personal Development Plan** introduced on pages 98-99 is a goal-setting worksheet and action plan. It is designed to map out specific learning objectives in the three profile categories (character, skills, and knowledge). This exercise may help you piece the tasks and growth areas you've noted on previous journal pages into a coherent whole.

Setting aside intentional time for personal growth and development should be a vital component of every missionary's ministry plan.

The Personal Development Plan can be used once to help you establish new direction for your own learning, or it can be adapted and used annually as a self-study guide to assist you as you analyze and shape your own lifelong learning process.

Coming up next are two short, practical exercises (in place of the journal worksheet in this section). You will want to work through these exercises to gain a clearer perspective on your past and to develop a personal growth plan for the future.

GAINING PERSPECTIVE: THE SYMBOL TIMELINE EXERCISE

Steve Hoke and Terry Walling

You may want to do this alone or in a small group of fellow pilgrims. Take a few minutes to depict your life pictorially, from birth to present, on a timeline. Use any symbols (figures, buildings, people, key words, etc.) that you find helpful to illustrate the progression of your personal journey. Include key people, circumstances, and events that have affected your development. Note significant dates and places, transitions, and changes.

After you complete your timeline, go to page 99 and complete the Personal Development Plan Worksheet.

PERSONAL TIMELINE

- -

Birth   Present

Upon completing your first draft, look back over your timeline to glean insights and convictions which can guide your development. What patterns do you see in your responsiveness to God? What major lessons has He taught you? In what situations have you learned the most about yourself? About God? About ministry?

Notice How...

• God has used key people, circumstances, and events (process items) to influence your development.

• Your life has gone through various phases or seasons of growth (development phases).

• Your life experiences, both positive and negative, have launched you to a greater level of growth and ministry. Many of these experiences serve to develop your life and ministry values.

This simple timeline should provide you with a big-picture view of your life and Christian growth. This perspective can give you new insights and encouragement about God's ongoing faithfulness and work in your life. It may also help you articulate to others how He has shaped your walk with Him thus far.

The Personal Development Plan (PDP)

Instructions: Work across each row of the chart on page 99 from left to right. Don't just write down stuff that's nice to know or that you want to learn. Focus on the specific training areas that relate to that dimension of formation (character qualities, ministry skills, or knowledge goals).

• Start by identifying your *developmental needs.* This will keep you focused on your "felt needs"—which is good, because you probably won't work at these skills unless you really think they're an area of need!

• Recording measurable *learning objectives* will help you identify specific "bytes" of growth that you can achieve. Describe them in a way that helps you think of ways to measure whether and how well you have accomplished them.

• Jot down *learning resources* that come to mind. If you're lacking information here, ask your pastor, friends, or mentor for additional ideas. Visiting a Christian bookstore should be enough to help you to identify a dozen books on just about any ministry topic. If you're on the field, talk with coworkers and network by e-mail with friends who may be knowledgeable about resources you could use.

> *Recording measurable learning objectives will help you identify specific "bytes" of growth that you can achieve.*

• Set realistic *dates for completion* in the timetable column. For example, don't try to complete all objectives by December 31; rather, spread them out over the course of the year so you'll always be working on something, yet won't be overwhelmed by everything at once.

• To increase the *accountability* factor, ask your pastor, field leader, mentor, or coach to look over and sign your plan. At a specified date, get back together and update him or her on how well you did.

Keeping It Current

Once you've written a PDP action plan, here are some suggestions for keeping it current:

• Revise and update your PDP annually, including specifics such as emphases for your quiet time and topics to study.

• Include reading goals. List the top 10-15 books you want to read each year. Read them in order of their importance to you.

• Stay in mentoring relationships for growth and accountability. Write in the names of your peer/relational mentors as well as selected "upward mentors."

PERSONAL DEVELOPMENT ACTION PLAN WORKSHEET FOR _____

ROLE: _____

DEVELOPMENT NEED What specific knowledge, attitude, skill, or character trait is needed? What results will be achieved by meeting this need?	OBJECTIVES/METHOD What measurable learning objectives (specific action steps) do you want to set for yourself to meet the development needs? What types of learning experiences will be most helpful? What types need to be designed?	RESOURCES Which coaches or mentors, books or materials, training courses, or experiences will be needed?	TIMETABLE When will action steps be taken?
Spiritual/Character Formation			
Ministry Skills			
Knowledge Goals			
Other			

Mentor's Signature _____ Date _____

Signature _____ Date _____

STEP 10: FINISHING STRONG

Bill Taylor

Those Old Shoes Still Do It for Me!

It's those old shoes that sit just to the left of my desk. I cannot avoid them. They stare at me, now dusty, at times dusted, now silent, now talking. They belong to an old marathoner friend of mine now living the last lap of a life fully lived. A few years ago I called him on the spur of the moment and asked him to send me a pair of his really old shoes. He cracked up laughing, asking why in the world I would request that. Simply, I said, "I want tangible shoe-leather evidence of how to finish well after all your years of life, marriage, parenting, cross-cultural ministry, leadership, laughing, loving, and serving."

So a few days later they arrived in a cardboard box. After unpacking them, I gazed at those cracked, worn symbols, thanking God for what they represented. This veteran began his marathon with Christ as a teen. He was the promise of his uncle's business in Atlanta, Georgia, until he informed his uncle that business was not his passion; Jesus was. The reprisal came rapidly; the angry uncle totally disinherited his nephew. Ironically, this action truly set him free for a God-driven future. The runner married a life partner in the Great Race, and together they began the marathon of life and ministry. Studies at Moody Bible Institute balanced with pastoral ministry in a Swedish Covenant Church in East Chicago, Indiana; a daughter came into their world; they were turned down by two (get it, two!) mission agencies for "health reasons." Enough to become a pre-attrition case of attrition! But these two runners persevered, and another sending body took them on in 1938. Following linguistic studies in the then-young Wycliffe Bible Translators program, they sailed for Latin America. A son was born soon after.

After a decade of service, they returned for further study at Wheaton College, sensing the need to upgrade their skill set and gift mix. Over the next decades, their Race took them to three Latin American countries for ministry, then 12 years as the CEO of the mission agency in the U.S. When this creative Runner approached his 60th birthday, he and his wife informed the mission board that they desired to return to field based ministry in Spain. They would serve under a much younger man whom the Runner years ago had recruited for Spain. The board was stunned, and the chairman admonished him, "Sir, no president of a bank ever returns to become a teller." To which the Runner quietly replied, "I do not work in a bank!"

They served/ran the Great Race in Spain for five years, developed a vibrant camp and conference center west of Madrid, turned it over to Spanish leaders, and then returned to the U.S. What now? These battle-worn veterans could have opted for retirement, but their spirits were strong and the body still had more laps to go. So they returned to their geographic roots and began planting Hispanic churches in the metropolitan Atlanta area. In God's goodness, now, about seven Spanish-speaking churches owe their existence to this vision.

But I'm most impressed with the deep character dynamics of this Runner. He had a unique combination of natural and spiritual abilities: visionary leadership and administrative gifts, coupled with spiritual insight and sensitive pastoral care. He was not threatened by younger or more brilliant leaders, and he opened space for them to emerge into responsibility. He mentored an unusual number of Latin American young leaders during his career. He recognized his wife's unusual gift blend and released her for complete

parallel fulfillment. He was a strong leader, but servant-hood marked his style.

Those old shoes. I cannot get away from them. This Runner now walks at a slow pace, as does his life partner in ministry. They are still deeply in love with each other, read actively, and now in their mid to late 80s stay active teaching weekly Bible classes. He recently told me that the two of them laugh a lot—at things, at each other, at other people.

Those old shoes talk to me, encouraging me, challenging me, saying, "Bill, finish well!" A postscript word to our readers: get your own pair of similar old shoes from someone finishing well the Great Race.

Why This Story of the Old Shoes?

I tell you this story because I personally need ongoing encouragement to keep my eyes on the Ultimate Goal, not the management goals of my organization, not the false, self-imposed goals of a society that values high productivity, measurable and tangible outcomes, an ever-increasing profile of apparent success (whether you get there by the humble route or not!). I pass on this account also because most of you are younger readers than Steve or I, and certainly much younger than my veteran friend, the Runner.

But all of us, men and women, need to be wary of the traps set out for us. Some of them will simply trip us up for a while, and we will recover, possibly through confession of sin and restoration, or simply through the natural path of maturation. But other traps are deadly and can destroy our lives and ministries, our integrity and our families.

So let's take a bold look at something that may be theory for many of you, namely, finishing well. But look at it this way: the least you can do right now is to anticipate the potential mine fields out there, discerning some of the dangers, and learning from those further along the race who have battled to finish well.

Two Case Studies From Scripture

Daniel, that great public servant, one of God's great tentmakers, was professionally agile enough to serve through at least five different despotic regimes. He almost sets our standard. Early in his forced international study program, living in exile, this brilliant youth made some radical choices. He purposed in his heart that he would not cave in to the cultural, religious, and power pressures of his world. It was a scary option, but having made that radical decision, God moved into the scenario, empowering him to keep his word. Even in his fading years, he remained faithful to those personal vows, and when he might legitimately have shaved his standards to avoid visiting hungry lions, he stayed firm. And for that reason the High God calls him "highly esteemed" (Dan. 10:11). Why? Because he finished well.

The Apostle Paul gives us another example, this time from prison: "I have fought the good fight, I have finished the race, I have kept the faith" (2 Tim. 4:7). Paul had lived long enough to see some of his friends and ministry colleagues somehow withdraw from the race. We don't know all of the reasons, although in some cases Paul hints at the root causes. But Paul passionately wanted to finish well, and he did—executed by the Roman Empire as a threat to the regal system.

Clarification: What Does Finishing Well Really Mean?

Finishing well does *not* mean someone who completes his or her personal career, regardless of the vocation, whether in ministry or not, on top of the "success pile" that is lauded by all as the great example of modern ministry production. Finishing well does not mean great banquets celebrating retirement, or biographies written about you, or going on the final conference circuit sharing your secrets to success, nor having your 10-step video programs dazzling millions. It does not mean prizes given to the spell-binding speakers, the writers of self-help books, the powerful motivational speakers, the evangelical celebrities, the prophetically gifted ones, the great public intercessors, the international missions mobilizers or legendary missionaries. Nor does it mean that the high prize is given to parents who claim, "I praise God that all my children are on fire for God and serving Him in...."

So what does finishing well really mean? It means coming to the end of the life race with integrity, not fame. I personally have two passions in life related to finishing well, and I measure them simply. Finishing well to me means ending with integrity towards my wife and my children. At my funeral I want my family to say, "Dad loved Mom passionately unto the end, was totally faithful to her, and did not sacrifice his children on an illegitimate altar of his traveling ministry." That's my bottom line.

The second passion is simply to do all I can to pack heaven with worshipers. Those two passions drive me to finish well.

Finishing well in cross-cultural ministry does not mean having to stay a missionary for the rest of your life, nor to base in the same geography all your life, regardless of your dreams or desires, or whether you are gifted for that task. The future missionary will serve with greater mobility, according to global and local needs, based on his or her skill set and gift mix, seeking to expand the kingdom into the tough unreached areas, and also committed to building up the church of Christ, wherever. The true meaning of the Great Commission equally balances the proclamation of the gospel and the edification of the church.

Finishing well is best done in community. That includes our extended family, our spiritual family, our church family, our colleagues in ministry, our fellow believers from different nations and cultures, and in particular those to whom we have entrusted our deeper life, our fellow mentors and intercessors. Finishing well also means completing in the right manner the different stages of our ministry and assignments, not just the Final Finish.

Finishing well means loving the Triune God with passion, even in the midst of pain and crushing disappointment, completing the race with integrity.

Too many of us have suffered from the image of the Christian life as the Summer Olympics. We honor and exult in those who jump the highest, run or swim the fastest, endure the most, and above all, those who get the gold medal. Who remembers any bronze medallists of any Olympics, much less those who finished last in any event? But it helps me so much to think of the Christian life as a lifelong pilgrimage, more akin to the Special Olympics. These latter games are great, because it does not really matter who wins, but that all who desire to compete are able to do so at some level. And as those runners and swimmers come close to the finish, arms and legs flailing in all directions, they cross to the cheer of the coach and crowd.

That's a better analogy for us. The Christian life is a Special Olympics, and the key is for each of us, regardless of age, gender, and vocation, to cross that final line, every appendage flailing in every which direction. But we have finished. And our Coach is there to welcome us and lead us in to the banquet.

Finishing well may mean completing life with broken dreams and unfulfilled desires, with children who may or may not be walking with Christ. It may mean that there are few obvious-to-the-world evidences of high production—particularly a problem for those of us who live in cultures that reward efficiency, effectiveness, and tangible, busy productivity. Finishing well means loving the Triune God with passion, even in the midst of pain and crushing disappointment, completing the race with integrity.

So Why Don't Many Finish Well?

We are told that a disturbing percentage of men and women in ministry, including missions, do not finish well. In my own research, buttressed by the more serious work of Bobby Clinton of Fuller Seminary, I've emerged with some observations on some of the major pitfalls that torpedo our path. Some have called these development stoppers; I call them traps.

As I list this series, check yourself out and attempt to discern where you might be vulnerable. Each of us has a weak side, and the sooner we recognize it and shore it up, the better off we are. You may say, "I'm too young for all of this to make sense, and it sounds so negative, so why waste my time here?" Well, let me assure you, this is no waste of time; but you may have to take that on faith from someone who has pilgrimaged further along the path and who has seen a lot along the way.

Some of the Major Traps

1. The trap of financial mismanagement, at times driven by ambition to acquire money by the wrong means. Watch out for money problems, particularly if you come from a background of poverty or the total opposite, high wealth, and now in ministry you are closer to poverty!

2. The trap of sexual temptation, whether as singles or marrieds. It's a danger for both women and men today as never before. Many of our younger missionaries come from broken families and have been sexually active prior to encountering Christ in power. Others have lived in a gay or lesbian lifestyle until set free by the power of God. Temptation patterns can re-emerge later in life and cause a fall. Married men tend to succumb to infidelity more than the wives, and the reasons are diverse. Not all marital infidelity leads to a broken family, but the broken trust is a tough one to rebuild.

3. Serious family problems, primarily due to an obvious lack of parental discipline of the children and worked out in their youth or to conflicts between husband and wife. The combination of these will torpedo ministry, for integrity is lost and the family simply neutralizes the gospel. This does *not* require perfect ministry families! Thank God!

At certain points in life, the Spirit will invite His servants into a deeper level of brokenness and suffering. This kind of testing can bring out the best or the worst in us.

---

4. The abuse of power in ministry. Most missionaries will not make much money, but many substitute that loss for an abuse of authority. It's difficult for them to submit to authority, and then when they get it, they will use it in a destructive way. And over time, many of you will emerge into leadership, for good or for ill.

5. Pride and ambition to "get to the top" of the ministry ladder. It's astonishing to observe the machinations—many times couched in the "language of humility"—that people will use to work their way into the high echelons of leadership and influence. The Apostle Peter had it right, "Humble yourselves, therefore, under God's mighty hand, that He may lift you up in due time" (1 Pet. 5:6).

6. The inability to turn over leadership and authority at the end of a service term, or at the conclusion of top leadership in the organization, or facing retirement. There are simply too many examples of men and women who won't let go! And the results are so clear, damaging so many individuals and organizations.

7. Testing in the middle of ministry is a unique case. After decades of studying God's ways in ministry, I have concluded that at certain points in life, the Spirit will invite His servants into a deeper level of brokenness and suffering. This may come from our sin, and we will deserve what God brings to us. But the brokenness may be a sovereign and yet complex invitation to walk in the broken path of Messiah. Why does God do this to us? I'm not sure, but I sense it's because He's in the process of purifying us, of preparing us for the next stage of ministry. Ironically, this next stage might mean ministry from the sidelines, away from the dangerous spotlight. It may mean we will end up walking with a kind of "life limp," reflecting the battle between Jacob and the angel (Gen. 32:22-32). I am astonished at that passage in Isaiah where it records that "it was the Lord's will to crush Him and cause Him to suffer" (Isa. 53:10). What mystery!

This kind of testing can bring out the best or the worst in us. For when God invites us into major brokenness, He will not force it upon us, but rather gives us the choice. If we say "no," His blessing is not fully removed, but one thing for sure, we will not be what we could have been in His original purpose of growth through suffering.

8. Coasting to the end is a peculiar pitfall, and it speaks of those who have simply run out of vital energy for the task and perhaps even more seriously, struggle with internal dry rot of the soul. So they maintain the systems, play the games, and go through the routines of ministry and spirituality. But their heart is not in it. And neither is the power of the Spirit present!

9. Spiritual warfare. We must be able to discern where our arch-enemy attacks us, and we must absolutely detect our personal, unique weak spots. They may have roots in our deep background, in biological factors, in personality weaknesses. But one thing you can be sure, the enemy will throw all he can at us to take us out.

What Are Some Antidotes?

Hey! There's good news out there. First of all, the High Triune God is on our side, His Spirit lives inside, and His Son advocates for us before the Father. But let me suggest some brief things to keep in mind. Incidentally, many of these were forged in the context of my years of cross-cultural ministry in Latin America.

1. Identify your personal weaknesses, of character and spirituality, and then shore them up. In my case, my wife knows these and strengthens me in my own battle.

2. Develop a sensitive heart to the terrible panoply of sin and the ways it appeals to you. But also grow a tender heart to the loving and sovereign Father, Son, and Spirit.

3. If you marry, never forget your vows. I made some big mistakes as a husband in my early years of ministry in Latin America. Fortunately, they were not major "sin" issues, but simply an unusual lack of sensitivity to my young bride struggling to learn a foreign language, live in a cross-cultural setting, grow in her own identity as a woman and as a woman in ministry, and balance the demands of small children with the expectations of "being a missionary." And I was a missionary kid who had returned "home," thus unable to enter into her struggles. So I learned some good lessons early on! There is no substitute for a husband (and vice versa) who enhances his wife as a person, partner, and daughter of the King.

4. Be wary of the seduction of travel invitations when you have children at home. I had to learn this also the hard way, but I am so thankful for the guidelines my wife and I developed early on to control these "glorious invitations to save the world." We also saw too many colleagues who were out there "doing their great thing" but losing their children or, worse, their spouse.

5. Grow an accountability community, whether of one key person or a small group. There is no need to have a large group for deep intimacy. Be careful with whom you share your deepest struggles, as not all people can handle such knowledge.

6. Be wary of the attacks of the enemy when you are alone, particularly when you travel in ministry. I prefer to have a colleague stay with me in a hotel room so we can help strengthen one another's resolve to avoid the dangerous TV programs and movies that rot the soul.

7. Ask God to help you develop a prayer shield of deep friends who will become serious intercessors for you. Some of these will stay with you all your life, but recognize that others will be with you only for a season.

8. Commit to building up your inner life of genuine spirituality. Select key writers who touch you deeply, but be wary of the press releases that tell you, "This is the book the church has waited to read for 2,000 years!" Go back to some of the spirituality classics, and drink deeply from them. A few contemporary writers have much to say to us. I personally have been radically shaped by A.W. Tozer, Henri Nouwen, and Eugene Peterson's books.

9. Never stop learning, reading, growing, studying, and expanding your horizons. If you are married, you can encourage each other to grow as you read and study. Develop a lifetime perspective on ministry and personal growth in Christ.

10. Commit to being mentored and to mentoring others. This is something we will develop further in this last chapter.

What About the Attrition of Missionaries?

I was involved in coordinating a 14-nation study of the attrition of long-term missionaries. And by attrition we mean all reasons for return from cross-cultural ministry. We discovered that approximately 5.1% of the long-term mission force leaves the field each year, and 71% of that figure leave for "preventable" reasons.

What does that mean? Let's estimate the current long-term, international, cross-cultural force at 150,000 strong. An annual loss of 5.1%

> *Approximately 5.1% of the long-term mission force leaves the field each year, and 71% of that figure leave for "preventable" reasons. This is an attrition of 21,726 long-term missionaries over a four-year term.*

means 7,650 missionaries leaving the field each year. Over a four-year term, this figure jumps to 30,600. This is the total loss for all reasons. The "preventable" percentage of 71% of that 30,600 gives us an attrition of 21,726 long-term missionaries over a four-year term. The dramatic statistic is heavy, the financial implications are striking and calculable, but the human implications are staggering. And we want to reduce this preventable attrition in all ways that we can. Even more important, you yourself don't want to be a future preventable attrition statistic!

There are a number of attrition categories here, with some overlap in the groups:

1. Normal, unavoidable, or expected attrition, such as death, retirement, or conclusion of a work contract or development project.

2. Unpreventable attrition, such as the issues related to the education of children, health reasons, a change of job with transfer to another ministry, conflicts within the family, or even diminished financial support.

> *We cannot underscore enough the importance of a strong church community for future missionaries.*

3. Preventable or painful reasons, such as some emotional or moral problem issues, lack of prayer or funding, miscommunications of job description and expectations, disagreement with the sending agency, conflicts with peers, lack of call, and inadequate pre-field training.

Significantly, the top reasons for field departure were markedly different for the older sending countries (OSC, which included the U.S., Canada, Germany, England, Australia, and Denmark) and the newer sending countries (NSC—Brazil, Costa Rica, Nigeria, Ghana, Philippines, Singapore, India, and Korea)

OSC Top Five
1. Normal retirement
2. Children
3. Change of job
4. Health problems
5. Lack of home support (finances and prayer)

NSC Top Five
1. Lack of home support (finances and prayer)
2. Lack of clear call
3. Inadequate commitment to the long haul
4. Disagreements with agency
5. Problems with peer missionaries

So How Can We Avoid Being a Future Attrition Statistic?

I've reviewed our previous nine chapters and realized that so much of what we have written is designed to avoid "preventable" or painful attrition. And the key is to grapple with these things prior to field departure. They have to do with character and spirituality issues, emotional maturity, the ability to serve creatively under authority, life in community, gifts that emerge and are tested and evaluated in the context of the local church, and completion of basic education. We cannot underscore enough the importance of a strong church community for future missionaries. The church is the missionary seedbed, the principal selector and screener, the fundamental equipper, the prime sender and intercessor base. Of course, the wise church will partner in pre-field training with specialized schools, and it should engage in a strategic partnership with a field based agency for proper supervision, shepherding, and strategizing.

Final Thoughts on Finishing Well

I primarily want to encourage you. I suspect that most of you (congratulations for having gotten this far with us!) will be younger disciples of the Risen Christ, and you are passionately committed to the cross-cultural telling of the Great Story. So it's possible that much of this chapter is theoretical. But it can potentially be one of the most significant chapters of the book, for it deals with the inner you, the long-distance pilgrimage race, hanging in with integrity until the end.

So be strong hearted; take cheer. We are with you! Oh, by the way, that veteran Runner? I called him the other day and checked up on them. We concluded the conversation with my words to him, "Dad, I really love you and Mom." Those old shoes mean a lot to me.

A PERSONAL CHECKLIST

1. Think through some of the people you know who are finishing well. _____
   _____

2. What lessons can you learn from their story? _____
   _____
   _____

3. How about some you know who have not finished well in their Christian life? _____
   _____

4. What were the primary causes that hindered them? _____
   _____

5. What can you learn from their negative stories for your own life? _____
   _____
   _____

6. Can you identify some of your own weaknesses that need to be shored up? _____
   _____

7. What might cause you to struggle with finishing well? _____
   _____
   _____

8. In what ways does the story of the veteran Runner and his shoes encourage you? _____
   _____

THE EFFECTIVENESS CHECKLIST

Terry Walling

The following checklist will help you evaluate your development in light of the five habits of effectiveness described below. After each statement, circle the number on the continuum that most accurately describes your current practice of that habit. Circle "0" if that habit is not present at all; circle "5" if you feel you are practicing that habit consistently with effectiveness.

	Very Poor					Excellent
1. Maintains a learning posture throughout life.	0	1	2	3	4	5
2. Committed to mentoring and being mentored.	0	1	2	3	4	5
3. Holds a dynamic ministry philosophy.	0	1	2	3	4	5
4. Engages in repeated times of personal renewal.	0	1	2	3	4	5
5. Has a lifetime perspective on ministry and development.	0	1	2	3	4	5

Total your score for the five habits.   Total: _____

Your score profiles your relative strengths and weaknesses in each of the habits. You should base your interpretation not on the total score, but on how your scores on each habit compare with each other. This can help you determine where you need to focus your efforts.

YOUR PERSONAL MISSION STATEMENT EXERCISE

Steve Hoke, Gary Mayes, and Terry Walling

Run water through a water pipe six feet in diameter and you have great volume with great potential. Force that same water through the nozzle of a fire hose and you have great impact.

You were created for a life that makes that kind of impact. You are being shaped and positioned by God Himself to make a unique contribution for the kingdom. The Apostle Paul said it this way, "For we are God's workmanship created in Christ Jesus to do good works, which *God prepared in advance* for us to do" (Eph. 2:10).

How do you discover what those "good works" are supposed to be? With all of the options for significant ministry, how do you discover nozzle-like focus for your life and ministry?

The series of exercises that leads to a personal mission statement will help you discover and articulate your unique contribution. At the core, a personal mission statement is all about destiny, and destiny is about living out God's purposes for your life.

What exactly is a personal mission statement? It is a dynamic statement that captures your best understanding to date of the unique contribution for which God has created you. Effective mission statements weave together your biblical purpose, life-ministry values, and personal vision.

How will a personal mission statement help you? A personal mission statement provides encouragement and fulfillment, helping a leader stay on track during times of stress or testing in ministry. It provides a decision-making grid that helps a leader assess various ministry opportunities. It points out areas where intentional growth and mentoring are needed to achieve full impact. And it serves as a personal call to arms, helping a leader stay mission minded amidst the plethora of daily distractions.

Creating your personal mission statement will involve tackling the following three focus questions and then weaving the three strands together.

1. Why do I exist? (biblical purpose)
2. How has God shaped me? (unique life-shaping and life-ministry values)
3. What is God calling me to accomplish? (vision)

> *A personal mission statement is a dynamic statement that captures your best understanding to date of the unique contribution for which God has created you.*

1. Why Do You Exist? (Your Biblical Purpose)

Biblical purpose articulates your best understanding of why you exist. It takes into account the mandates of Scripture and then captures in your own words what you believe about the life God created you to live.

What has God taught you? What verses has God used to shape your sense of purpose in life, verses that now serve like a compass, keeping you on the right track?

Personal reflection. Write a response to the following prompt questions to help you begin personalizing your thoughts about biblical purpose.

- Why did God create me? Why do I exist as a person?
- What does God say should provide my greatest joy?
- What is my response to God's work of grace and salvation on my behalf?
- What is my personal response to the Lordship of Christ?

Scripture search. Push your reflections a bit further by reviewing the verses listed below. Read each passage and write out your response to the question, "What insights does this passage provide regarding the purpose of my life from God's perspective?"

Scripture   Insight

Matthew 16:24-26

Matthew 22:37-40

Matthew 28:18-20

John 13:34-35

Romans 15:6-7

Ephesians 2:8-10

Philippians 3:7-14

2 Timothy 1:9

1 Peter 2:1-5

2 Peter 1:5-9

Your biblical purpose. Based on your understanding of Scripture and your reflections above, write out what you perceive to be your biblical purpose. A healthy biblical purpose statement should be concise and reflect the biblical mandate that we have as believers. While your understanding of biblical purpose may apply to all believers, the way you express it should be personally significant to you.

My biblical purpose: _____

_____

_____

_____

2. How Has God Shaped You?
(Your Unique Shaping and Life-Ministry Values)

The next step in developing your personal mission statement is to reflect on your unique shaping as a leader. Life-ministry values are the key to understanding this unique shaping.

Life-ministry values are the beliefs, assumptions, and preferences that guide your behavior and actions. Values often show up first as lessons or beliefs, but they are forged into core convictions through experience, often the painful kind. While there are many things we may identify as generally true or important, our core values shape actual and ongoing behavior.

Life-ministry values should encompass:
- Your personal journey with Christ.
- Family, relationships, and accountability.
- Biblical convictions and principles.
- Insights concerning ministry and mission.
- Insights related to leadership.
- Character formation and effectiveness.
- Unique calling and contribution.

As you think about the priorities and convictions that guide your life and ministry, you will want to identify 6-10 values in regard to the topics above. Capture each in one or two words and then describe them concisely.

Examples of life-ministry value statements:
- Kingdom: I value the kingdom, not just local church growth.
- The church: I value the primacy of the church as God's vehicle of mission in the world.
- Change: I value change, helping the church and God's people move forward.
- Teamwork: I value people, team ministry, and relational empowerment.

Write out your values. Using the space below, write out your values. Work hard to keep your value statements concise and direct (ideally, 10 words or less).

	Key Word(s)	Life-Ministry Value Statement
1.		
2.		
3.		
4.		

3. What Is God Calling You to Accomplish? (Vision for Your Personal Life and Ministry)

Vision—*the ability to see God's preferable future*—is the heartbeat of the personal mission statement. Vision is a word picture that describes what you believe God desires to accomplish. It flows from the heart of God as He invites us to participate in the redemptive work of His kingdom. Our task is neither to invent the future nor our calling; our task is to discover what God is doing and join Him in it. Vision describes that work.

Vision involves passion! It motivates and captivates the leader. It is what the heart yearns to see accomplished. Healthy vision is specific, not general. Personal vision answers this question: If you knew that you would not fail, what would you do, in your lifetime, for the glory of God?

Discovering your personal vision. The following questions provide multiple lenses into the things God has stirred inside of you. Answer each question and allow them to stimulate fresh thinking about your own vision.

1. The people and circumstances that have most shaped my life are… _____

_____

_____

2. When I think about ministry in the future, the area of ministry I would love to concentrate upon is… _____

_____

_____

3. The qualities of character I most admire and desire for God to shape into my life include the following: _____

_____

_____

4. People who know me believe I am most used by God when I am involved in… _____

Why? _____

5. My ministry activities that contribute most to God's kingdom are… _____

Why? _____

_____

6. When people talk about passion for ministry, I often begin to think about giving my life to accomplishing… ____

Why? _____

_____

Based on the way God has shaped you in your past, your reflections above, and your passion for ministry, write out your answer to the question: *If you knew you would not fail, what would you do, in your lifetime, for the glory of God?*

_____

_____

_____

_____

_____

Vision is often the hardest of the three components of personal mission to articulate. Typically, we know the most about biblical purpose, some about life-ministry values, and the least about personal vision.

Ask these questions as a means of sharpening your work on vision.

• Can you see it? (True vision is a word picture that describes what God will accomplish. The more vague it is, the less motivating.)

• Is it bigger than you? (Godly vision demands faith, and faith implies risk.)

• Is it anchored to God's work in your past?

• Does it engage your passion?

• Would you do it if you didn't get paid, or would you pay for the chance to do it?

Weaving It All Together

Your Personal Mission Statement

You are ready to put the pieces together. A personal mission statement is the interweaving of your *biblical purpose*, your *life-ministry values*, and your *personal vision*. Using the work you have done, blend together these three elements into one comprehensive statement. It should be no longer than two or three paragraphs.

A Suggested Method

1. Begin on another piece of paper.
2. At the top of the paper write down your biblical purpose.
3. Skip a line or two and write down your personal vision.
4. Now attempt to weave your values into these other two components as modifiers and clarifiers, personalizing what your contribution looks like. This integration will give the document passion and make it uniquely personal.
5. Make a copy and keep it with you for daily reference.

FINDING PERSONAL MENTORS EXERCISE

Steve Hoke and Terry Walling

By this point you have clarified your past shaping and processing by drawing your *personal timeline*. You have sharpened your future direction with the development of your *personal mission statement*. The final question is: Who will help you accomplish your mission?

Are you looking for a person who can give you perspective and provide wisdom, support, resources, and guidance as you seek to grow and develop into the person and leader that God intends? Do you desire to help others grow and achieve a level of effectiveness that they have yet to experience? Do you desire to influence the next generation of Christian leaders?

What Is Mentoring?

Mentoring links leaders to the resources of others, empowering them for greater personal growth and ministry effectiveness. Mentoring is "a relational experience in which one person empowers another by sharing God-given resources" (Stanley and Clinton, *Connecting*, p. 33). Mentoring is making the mentor's personal strengths, resources, and networks (friendships/contacts) available to help a protégé (mentoree) reach his or her goals.

Mentoring links leaders to the resources of others, empowering them for greater personal growth and ministry effectiveness.

The mentor is the person who shares the God-given resources. The mentoree is the person being empowered. The interactional transfer between the mentor and mentoree is called empowerment.

Mentors offer empowerment resources. The relationship between mentor and mentoree may be formal or informal, scheduled or sporadic. The exchange of resources may take place over a long time or just once. Such empowerment usually occurs face to face, but it may happen over a great distance (especially today using telephone, fax, and e-mail).

- Mentors empower mentorees with encouragement and timely advice gained through life and ministry experience.
- Mentors model habits of leadership and ministry and challenge mentorees to gain broader perspectives and new maturity. These lessons build confidence and credibility in mentorees.
- Mentors link mentorees with important resources, such as books, articles, people, workshops, financial resources, and opportunities to minister with the mentor.

Three Kinds of Mentoring

"Christian workers need relationships that will mentor us, peers who will co-mentor us, and people that we are mentoring. This will help ensure a balanced and healthy perspective on life and ministry," says J. Robert Clinton in *Please Mentor Me*. Lifelong leadership development is greatly enhanced by a balance of three kinds of mentoring relationships—upward mentoring, co-mentoring (internal and external), and disciple mentoring (see the sample mentoring constellation below).

Upward mentoring pushes leaders forward to expand their potential. Upward mentors are typically older, more mature Christian leaders who see the bigger picture and how a leader's current situation fits into that picture. Their experience and knowledge base is more advanced than that of the mentoree. They give valuable advice and challenge the mentoree to persevere and grow.

Co-mentoring is along-side mentoring that comes from peers who are either inside or outside a leader's daily frame of reference.

Internal co-mentors are peers in your ministry environment who are at approximately the same level of spiritual maturity. They provide mutual growth and accountability, contextual insights within the organization, and friendship during difficulty.

External co-mentors, because they are outside your ministry situation, can provide an objective perspective and can challenge your thinking and acting.

Disciple mentoring means empowering younger or less experienced leaders. It involves you in the lives of emerging leaders whom you need to identify, select, and help develop. In these relationships you provide accountability, challenge, insight, and critical skills for new leaders.

Sample Mentoring Constellation

The following example shows the three kinds of mentoring and the types of mentors* that can guide your development:

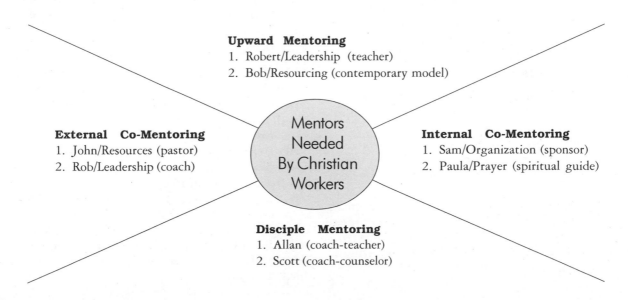

Upward Mentoring
1. Robert/Leadership (teacher)
2. Bob/Resourcing (contemporary model)

External Co-Mentoring
1. John/Resources (pastor)
2. Rob/Leadership (coach)

Mentors Needed By Christian Workers

Internal Co-Mentoring
1. Sam/Organization (sponsor)
2. Paula/Prayer (spiritual guide)

Disciple Mentoring
1. Allan (coach-teacher)
2. Scott (coach-counselor)

---

* Check out Terry Walling's *Finding Personal Mentors* workbook (Carol Stream, IL: CRM Publishing/ChurchSmart Resources, 1996) for a fuller discussion of terms and types of mentors.

Leaders don't always have mentors for all the quadrants. That is normal. But long-term lack of one type of mentoring is dangerous. Begin praying for balance in the mentors God will give you.

Finding Personal Mentors

Initiating the mentor relationship is most often up to you, the mentoree. Reflect on the following questions as you begin looking for the right mentors in your life:

• What type of help do you feel you need most?

• What are your mentoring issues (needs)?

List at least three prioritized goals for your life and ministry for the next year. Next to each goal, list the name of a potential mentor. Then plot your potential candidates on the mentoring constellation below.

Life Development Goals	Potential Mentors
1.	
2.	
3.	

Ministry Development Goals	Potential Mentors
1.	
2.	
3.	

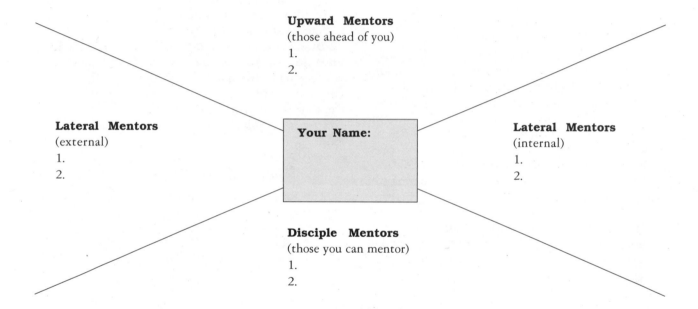

Upward Mentors
(those ahead of you)
1.
2.

Lateral Mentors
(external)
1.
2.

Your Name:

Lateral Mentors
(internal)
1.
2.

Disciple Mentors
(those you can mentor)
1.
2.

Guidelines for Mentoring Relationships

The "Ten Commandments of Mentoring," developed by Paul Stanley and Bobby Clinton in their book, *Connecting*, will help guide your mentoring relationships to greater effectiveness. Use these first five as a general guide, but don't let the relational aspects be hampered by too much formality.

1. Establish the relationship. Sometimes mentoring relationships just happen. Sometimes they are developed intentionally and cultivated. Mentoring has a better chance for empowerment when a relationship is clearly established.

2. Jointly agree on the purpose of the mentoring relationship. By spelling out the expectations, you can avoid unfulfilled expectations and disappointments.

3. Determine how often you will meet.

4. Determine the nature of accountability. Agree together on how the accountability will be set up and monitored. You can use written reports, phone calls, or general verbal feedback.

5. Set up clear lines of communication. Discuss when, how often, and by what means you will interact. Also discuss the freedom on behalf of both persons in questioning and discussing topics.

OUR LAST WORDS AND YOUR NEXT STEPS

Looking Back and Moving Ahead

Steve Hoke and Bill Taylor

Well, that's just about it. You have seriously embarked upon the process of charting your own journey to the nations. If you've made it this far, it's been by faith, hard work, and endurance. Congratulations! You are to be commended!

We trust that as you've worked through the counsel in this book and taken the first steps toward reaching the nations for Christ, you have grown in substantial ways—in your character, in your church base, in your ministry effectiveness, and in your overall knowledge. We really hope that you've seen your destiny defined and have felt God's empowering presence as you step out in obedient faith. You certainly have enough contact addresses, Web pages, and further resources to keep you going for a while!

Maybe you haven't always known exactly where you were going, but you've been keenly aware of God's guiding presence with you. You've sensed God's touch in your life, either lightly or strongly. You've seen tangible answers to prayer, and perhaps some prayers that were not answered. You're able to deal with a bit more ambiguity in life and the life in Christ. You've possibly already experienced some painful failures in your personal life as well as in relationships and even in ministry. That's all part of the package of discipleship. You've experienced some divine encounters with God and perhaps with some other people. You've entered into a mentoring relationship that is giving you substantial input and counsel.

Overall, we trust that you have made definite progress in your journey toward active long-term service to Christ in the vast unevangelized parts of the world. Or perhaps the Lord has confirmed your role in another region of the huge world of human and spiritual needs where your precise gift mix and skill set will be used best. But wherever you are at this point, our prayer is that you will stay focused on knowing God and on building His cross-cultural kingdom by showing His love in practical ways, by making disciples, and by planting churches. As you go, we hope you will grow stronger with that high goal of finishing well—whether in your home country or in an adopted one.

The journey of faith is a lifelong process. God's pattern for working with His people is to develop them over the course of a lifetime. That's why the Christian life is best described as a lifelong pilgrimage. You will be tempted to get discouraged; you will be tempted to sin, to quit, to throw in the towel. You will meet lovely and apparently peaceful Hindus, Buddhists, Muslims. And these relationships may open an internal warfare as you battle with profound spiritual doubt, even wondering whether it's necessary to claim that Jesus is unique over the other faith systems.

You will be heartbroken when apparent believers slip away from Jesus. You may get sick, worse than you ever imagined you could, even wanting to die and get it over with! Hey, that's part of the deal. Remember Jesus! But when the temptations come to chuck it in, remember also that your ultimate desire is to love and honor the High Triune God.

> When the temptations come to chuck it in, remember also that your ultimate desire is to love and honor the High Triune God.

Most of you will start your global race strong, and the majority of you are young (at least younger than Steve and I—but then it's pretty easy to be younger than we are!). Begin your race with commitment and determination, and continue with patient endurance (Rev. 14:12) as the decades roll by. Some of you may serve for five years in cross-cultural ministry, then return "home" radically changed and forever internationalized.

Others will "sign up" for further terms, extending your ministry segment by segment. The most important thing is not where you geographically work out your discipleship to Jesus, but the reality that you pursue Him passionately, wherever. So stay focused for the distance, and get ready to be amazed as God brings glory to His name, and rejoice when it happens that He invites you to be a part of it. Enjoy your seasons among the people of every nation, tribe, and language who will one day worship together with you around the great throne of heaven.

Now that's a vision worth living and dying for!

Appendices

APPENDIX 1:
MODELS OF MISSION CAREER PATHS OF CHURCHES AND AGENCIES

TRAINING PATH: CHRISTIAN & MISSIONARY ALLIANCE (C&MA) (Colorado Springs, Colorado)

The Christian & Missionary Alliance began as a sending agency and now shows all the characteristics of a sending denomination. It provides a broad range of service opportunities (church planting, theological education, theological education by extension (TEE), evangelism, national church support, and relief aid), but emphasizes the sending of career missionaries related to C&MA churches. It has over 800 missionaries serving in 42 countries.

Phase 1: Getting Ready

PERSONAL SPIRITUAL FORMATION	ON-THE-JOB EXPERIENCE AT HOME	EXPOSURE TO OTHER CULTURES	BASIC EDUCATION
Conversion, personal spiritual walk, and witness examined.	Church membership and involvement required. At least 2 years home ministry experience required.	Alliance Youth Corps or short-term ministry experience overseas, or intercultural ministry experience in homeland.	College degree. At least 1 year of grad study at ATS or CTS, or approved equivalent. Min: 30 hours Bible and theology; at least 1 year at a C&MA school.

Phase 2: Getting There

AGENCY CONTACT AND CANDIDACY	MINISTRY ASSIGNMENT SEARCH	HANDS-ON MISSIONARY TRAINING
"Applicant" at undergraduate level. "Accredited candidate" at graduate level. "Appointment" on completion of home service.	Tentative field (country) assignment during formal training. Actual field assignment at appointment.	Pre-field orientation and second language acquisition program before departure.

Phase 3: Getting Established

APPRENTICESHIP/ INTERNSHIP	LIFELONG LEARNING	FINISHING STRONG
Initial 2 years on field in language and culture. Learning through mentoring by experienced missionaries.	Development programs provided on field and during home assignment. Specialized training based on field needs.	Career orientation assumed with appropriate member and family care program in place. Ministry assignments based on field strategy with sensitivity to individual abilities and experience. Ongoing accountability and evaluation provided.

TRAINING PATH: CHURCH RESOURCE MINISTRIES (CRM) (Anaheim, California)

CRM's mission is to develop leaders to strengthen and start churches worldwide. Founded in 1980, CRM is transdenominational, with over 200 staff working across North America and in over 10 countries internationally.

Phase 1: Getting Ready

PERSONAL SPIRITUAL FORMATION	ON-THE-JOB EXPERIENCE AT HOME	EXPOSURE TO OTHER CULTURES	BASIC EDUCATION
Maturing Christian walk. Growing in spiritual disciplines, especially Bible study, intercession, fasting, and meditation.	Actively involved with spiritual gifts in local church. Developing heart for and skills in evangelism, disciple-making, and growing and multiplying cell-groups.	One or more short-term ministry experiences preferred. Language aptitude and proficiency highly valued.	College degree required. Many staff have graduate work and degrees in specialty area(s).

Phase 2: Getting There

AGENCY CONTACT AND CANDIDACY	MINISTRY ASSIGNMENT SEARCH	HANDS-ON MISSIONARY TRAINING
Very open to phone, mail, or e-mail inquiries. Most staff come from personal contact of staff and referrals from churches.	Explore candidates' sense of call and gifting with them. Help them find best country/people group "fit" for them in consultation with field team. Visits to possible fields are encouraged.	MTI's 3-week pre-field orientation required, plus LAMP or MTI's language acquisition training. Prefer some cultural anthropology.

Phase 3: Getting Established

APPRENTICESHIP/ INTERNSHIP	LIFELONG LEARNING	FINISHING STRONG
All new staff serve 1 year apprenticeship during first year on field under team director or best mentor. Each staff urged to find multiple mentors. Staff evaluated regularly by team leader.	Each staff encouraged to pursue lifelong learning. All staff complete annual "Personal Development Plan" growth plans; evaluated semi-annually with director.	Staff are developmentally nurtured towards goal of finishing well and are mentored throughout tenure with CRM. Mid-career assessment offered to refocus staff when desired. Staff are helped to focus on unique contribution and unique methodology.

TRAINING PATH: CONSERVATIVE BAPTIST INTERNATIONAL (CBI) (Carol Stream, Illinois)

CBI is an evangelical sending agency of Baptist tradition engaged in church planting, evangelism, leadership development, theological education by extension (TEE), and literature production/distribution. It has over 600 missionaries in 43 countries.

Phase 1: Getting Ready

PERSONAL SPIRITUAL FORMATION	ON-THE-JOB EXPERIENCE AT HOME	EXPOSURE TO OTHER CULTURES	BASIC EDUCATION
Selection experience. Evidence of spiritual growth and discipline.	Church membership required, not necessarily Conservative Baptist. Active participation in church ministry.	Summer youth programs and short-term ministry opportunities recommended.	30 semester hours of Bible; undergraduate degree; seminary training (optional for some ministries).

Phase 2: Getting There

AGENCY CONTACT AND CANDIDACY	MINISTRY ASSIGNMENT SEARCH	HANDS-ON MISSIONARY TRAINING
Mobilization Department; Appointee.	Field chosen cooperatively by candidate and CBI in reference to field requests.	Orientation; summer cross-cultural training in inner city; language orientation.

Phase 3: Getting Established

APPRENTICESHIP/ INTERNSHIP	LIFELONG LEARNING	FINISHING STRONG
Language/culture learning. Partner with senior missionary.	Development of educational opportunities during Stateside leave by request and approval.	Focused goals and annual evaluation. Accountability to team members in ministry.

TRAINING PATH: EVANGELICAL FREE CHURCH MISSION (EFCM) (Minneapolis, Minnesota)

The EFCM is the mission arm of the Evangelical Free Church of America (EFCA) denomination, now numbering 1,250 churches across America, with 550 missionaries in 35 countries. The Free Church deploys teams focused on church planting in urban areas and among unreached people groups.

Phase 1: Getting Ready

PERSONAL SPIRITUAL FORMATION	ON-THE-JOB EXPERIENCE AT HOME	EXPOSURE TO OTHER CULTURES	BASIC EDUCATION
Know Christ in a personal way. Learn how to feed yourself spiritually. Learn how to share your faith.	Become active in a local church. Get experience there in discipling new Christians. Get experience there in leading small-group Bible studies.	Become involved in a cross-cultural ministry in U.S. Make at least one short-term missions trip internationally.	Traditional path: university>seminary> local church experience. Alternative path A: Bible college>local church experience. Alternative path B: Local church experience; distance learning concurrent with local church experience.

Phase 2: Getting There

AGENCY CONTACT AND CANDIDACY	MINISTRY ASSIGNMENT SEARCH	HANDS-ON MISSIONARY TRAINING
Meet representatives of EFCM. Complete preliminary question-naire and resume. Local church contacted for approval. Complete 2-stage application form. Day of interviews followed by 3 days of orientation.	EFCM representative listens to candidate and local church on ministry assignment. Mission sends information on candidate to pos-sible field to find right country and fit. Candidate dialogues with field leadership to confirm placement. Candidate takes "Ministry Match" test. May visit field of choice.	Through local church, educational institutions (see Basic Education), EFCM's 2 week candidate school, and MTI's Program in Language Acquisition Techniques and other specialized seminars offered by EFCM and various organizations.

Phase 3: Getting Established

APPRENTICESHIP/ INTERNSHIP	LIFELONG LEARNING	FINISHING STRONG
1-2 years of language study on field. 1-2 years of internship under experienced missionary church planter or national pastor. Regular evaluation by EFCM leadership. Occasional visits of "pastors to missionaries."	Church planting school offered regularly throughout career. Specialized seminars and advanced education on each home assignment as deemed necessary by missionary and field. Reentry seminar each term. Opportunity for more responsibility as readi-ness is indicated.	Commitment to lifetime personal ministry development. Finally, retirement planning seminar.

TRAINING PATH: FRONTIERS (Mesa, Arizona)

Frontiers is an international mission agency which is committed to establishing vital Christ-honoring churches among the world's 1 billion Muslims. Currently over 500 Frontiers missionaries serve on 81 church planting teams in 37 limited-access Muslim countries.

Phase 1: Getting Ready

PERSONAL SPIRITUAL FORMATION

Personal Christian commitment evidenced in a strong walk of faith.

ON-THE-JOB EXPERIENCE AT HOME

Strong sending church required and ministry experience desired.

EXPOSURE TO OTHER CULTURES

Not essential, but ethnophobes need not apply.

BASIC EDUCATION

Attitude of a learner essential with formal education welcomed.

Phase 2: Getting There

AGENCY CONTACT AND CANDIDACY

Call 1-800-GO-2-THEM and ask.

MINISTRY ASSIGNMENT SEARCH

Upon completion of preliminary application, contact with team leader will be established.

HANDS-ON MISSIONARY TRAINING

2-week candidate school required; additional training dependent upon assignment.

Phase 3: Getting Established

APPRENTICESHIP/ INTERNSHIP

Initially assigned to a team for language learning and internship.

LIFELONG LEARNING

Visible signs of continued learning and upgrading churches established.

FINISHING STRONG

Exiting people group; pioneering new work among new people group.

TRAINING PATH: MISSION TO THE WORLD (MTW) (Atlanta, Georgia)

Mission to the World is the mission arm of the Presbyterian Church in America (PCA) denomination, with over 550 career and two-year missionaries serving in 60 countries. The mission's focus is on church planting, evangelism, and support of national workers. They send people who are members of the PCA.

Phase 1: Getting Ready

PERSONAL SPIRITUAL FORMATION

Mature, growing Christian. Consistent in Bible study, prayer, fellowship, and ministry. Discipled in the area of missions by local church.

ON-THE-JOB EXPERIENCE AT HOME

Active member of a local PCA church. Ministry experience in the areas of evangelism and discipleship. Recommended by local church leadership for service overseas.

EXPOSURE TO OTHER CULTURES

Participation in an MTW or other short-term missions experience. Familiar with ministry of MTW missionaries from home church. Involved with internationals in the States where possible.

BASIC EDUCATION

College education or training and experience in a specialized skill. Advanced theological training not required unless placed as a pastor or theological educator.

Phase 2: Getting There

AGENCY CONTACT AND CANDIDACY

Discussion of interest with mission leaders in local church. Initial conversations. Complete application materials for MTW. Telephone interview. Assessment center (for church planters). Final interview with committee. Support team development.

MINISTRY ASSIGNMENT SEARCH

Placements must be confirmed before final interview. Factors considered in firming placement: Candidate's sense of call to particular location or people, MTW's current personnel needs; invitations by local MTW church planting team.

HANDS-ON MISSIONARY TRAINING

Customized pre-field training focusing on spiritual development, ministry skills, and cross-cultural adjustment. Elements depend on the particular placement and past experience and training of the candidate.

Phase 3: Getting Established

APPRENTICESHIP/ INTERNSHIP

2-year Impact program available for those wanting initial exposure to overseas ministry. Language training for longer term workers and as needed for 2-year missionaries.

LIFELONG LEARNING

Encouraged to continue education in various ways. Career development notebook provided for 2-year missionaries. Career missionaries can raise funds for further education on home assignment. Periodic field conferences and leadership training. Reentry seminar provided each furlough.

FINISHING STRONG

Debriefing process after each term, including time with Christian counselors. Regular evaluation on field by team leader. Reassignment to new fields available once work is completed. Annuity provided for career missionaries.

TRAINING PATH: OPERATION MOBILIZATION (OM) (Tyrone, Georgia)

An interdenominational sending agency of evangelical tradition engaged in evangelism, church planting, literature distribution, mobilization for training, and training. Their mission is to motivate, develop, and equip people for world evangelization, and to strengthen and help plant churches, especially among the unreached in the Middle East, South and Central Asia, and Europe.

Phase 1: Getting Ready

PERSONAL SPIRITUAL FORMATION	ON-THE-JOB EXPERIENCE AT HOME	EXPOSURE TO OTHER CULTURES	BASIC EDUCATION
Christian for 1 year. At least 17 years old. Consistent in Bible reading, prayer, fellowship, and witness.	Active in local church ministries. Recommended by local church.	Preferable, but not required.	High school or GED.

Phase 2: Getting There

AGENCY CONTACT AND CANDIDACY	MINISTRY ASSIGNMENT SEARCH	HANDS-ON MISSIONARY TRAINING
Preliminary application. Full application. Attend orientation conference. Interview. Support team building.	Placement determined by interest in location/vocation and needs of field.	Some fields have pre-field and on-field training, including language. Other fields provide hands-on training in evangelism, discipleship, leadership, etc.

Phase 3: Getting Established

APPRENTICESHIP/ INTERNSHIP	LIFELONG LEARNING	FINISHING STRONG
Ministry takes place in multicultural teams.	Encouraged for all members; some return for formal education/training.	Regular breaks. Home assignments are a part of ministry.

TRAINING PATH: OVERSEAS MISSIONARY FELLOWSHIP (OMF) (Littleton, Colorado)

Founded by Hudson Taylor as the China Inland Mission (CIM), OMF is an international, interdenominational agency focused on evangelism and church planting throughout Asia. They currently have 1,000 missionaries from 21 countries serving in 16 nations in Asia.

Phase 1: Getting Ready

PERSONAL SPIRITUAL FORMATION	ON-THE-JOB EXPERIENCE AT HOME	EXPOSURE TO OTHER CULTURES	BASIC EDUCATION
Know Christ. Rich devotional life. Evidence of spiritual and emotional growth and maturity.	Sent by local church. Ministry experience in church or on campus. Fruitful in ministry.	Cross-cultural short term or working with internationals in U.S. recommended.	Usually undergraduate degree; Bible/theological training appropriate to expected ministry.

Phase 2: Getting There

AGENCY CONTACT AND CANDIDACY	MINISTRY ASSIGNMENT SEARCH	HANDS-ON MISSIONARY TRAINING
Preliminary information form. Personal interview. Full application. Candidate course.	During application process identify interest in type of ministry, country, or people group. East Asia focus.	Pre-field orientation. On-field orientation. Language/culture learning. Ministry training.

Phase 3: Getting Established

APPRENTICESHIP/ INTERNSHIP	LIFELONG LEARNING	FINISHING STRONG
Initial term has learning emphasis. Usually mentor relationship with experienced workers.	Life and ministry development program. Home assignment institute. Continuing education encouraged.	Life and ministry development program. Assessment and review. Accountability.

TRAINING PATH: SIM INTERNATIONAL (Charlotte, North Carolina)

SIM International is an interdenominational agency focused on evangelism and church planting primarily across Africa, Asia, and Latin America, with over 1,300 missionaries serving in 35 countries.

Phase 1: Getting Ready

PERSONAL SPIRITUAL FORMATION	ON-THE-JOB EXPERIENCE AT HOME	EXPOSURE TO OTHER CULTURES	BASIC EDUCATION
Personal salvation experience. Clear commitment to missions. Demonstrated Christian character.	Proven ministry in the local church. Sending church's recognition of call and gifts.	Normally expect at least one short-term experience. Ideally involvement in cross-cultural relationships in the States.	College graduate; 30 hours of Bible and missions. Depending on place, post-graduate study necessary.

Phase 2: Getting There

AGENCY CONTACT AND CANDIDACY	MINISTRY ASSIGNMENT SEARCH	HANDS-ON MISSIONARY TRAINING
Application and references. Personality and psychological testing. Pre-orientation assessment. Orientation (1 month).	Career track chosen. Vocation. People group. Country.	Depending on placement, certain training such as survival, Muslim, language, various internships, local ethnic focus ministry.

Phase 3: Getting Established

APPRENTICESHIP/ INTERNSHIP	LIFELONG LEARNING	FINISHING STRONG
Normally under the supervision of an experienced missionary or national church leader. Language and culture learning.	At present, dictated by career track and missionary initiative. Projected: Mission leadership development for each member.	We provide opportunities for counseling, training, and continuing education with some intentional mentoring.

TRAINING PATH: WYCLIFFE BIBLE TRANSLATORS (WBT) (Orlando, Florida)

The Wycliffe Bible Translators, affiliated with the Summer Institute of Linguistics, is an example of the specialized career associated with single-purpose sending agencies. To a degree it represents the so-called faith missions in its expectation that all members (language related and support) are responsible to raise their own support.

Phase 1: Getting Ready

PERSONAL SPIRITUAL FORMATION	ON-THE-JOB EXPERIENCE AT HOME	EXPOSURE TO OTHER CULTURES	BASIC EDUCATION
Christian experience and commitment expected.	Must be under church care. Experience required for support role.	Helpful, not required.	College (not required for some support roles). Post-grad hoped for and welcomed.

Phase 2: Getting There

AGENCY CONTACT AND CANDIDACY	MINISTRY ASSIGNMENT SEARCH	HANDS-ON MISSIONARY TRAINING
Application usually made at some point in previous step.	Career track chosen. Vocation. People group. Country.	Essence of career. Basic and advanced course— 7-15 weeks. Orientation and cross-cultural training.

Phase 3: Getting Established

APPRENTICESHIP/ INTERNSHIP	LIFELONG LEARNING	FINISHING STRONG
First term considered part of training. Able to teach others.	Keyed to expected redeployment for further translation or other assignment, for translators.	

TRAINING PATH: YOUTH WITH A MISSION (YWAM) (Salem, Oregon)

YWAM is an international, interdenominational agency with over 9,500 staff serving in over 132 countries. Their focus is providing opportunities for short- and long-term cross-cultural service in evangelism, discipleship, church planting, compassion and development ministries, King's Kids, as well as early childhood education.

Phase 1: Getting Ready

PERSONAL SPIRITUAL FORMATION	ON-THE-JOB EXPERIENCE AT HOME	EXPOSURE TO OTHER CULTURES	BASIC EDUCATION
Personal wholeness. Teaching/training. Disciplines of prayer, worship, and Bible meditation learned.	Participates in local church. Ministry opportunities. Intercessory prayer. Participation and experience in leading small groups.	10- to 12-week outreaches or short-term outreaches year round.	High school for admission to training schools. Any age for short-term ministries.

Phase 2: Getting There

AGENCY CONTACT AND CANDIDACY	MINISTRY ASSIGNMENT SEARCH	HANDS-ON MISSIONARY TRAINING
Contact YWAM North America office: 7085 Battlecreek Rd. SE Salem, OR 97301	Review opportunities with staff person or personal spiritual advisors.	Supervised outreaches following DTS or SOE.

Phase 3: Getting Established

APPRENTICESHIP/ INTERNSHIP	LIFELONG LEARNING	FINISHING STRONG
Joining a staff position for 2 years.	Commitment to missions, either domestic or international, for 2 years.	Know the Lord in a deeper way. Make disciples wherever God calls.

TRAINING PATH: CEDAR SPRINGS PRESBYTERIAN CHURCH (PCA) (Knoxville, Tennessee)

Cedar Springs' world missions outreach has grown from three missionaries supported by a faith promise budget of $6,000 in 1974 to 106 missionary units and over 40 organizations with total missions giving for world evangelization of nearly $2 million in 1998. U.S. missions are supported from the church's General Fund. The church adopted five unreached people groups in 1994 and has seen a significant advance of the gospel in two of these.

Phase 1: Getting Ready

PERSONAL SPIRITUAL FORMATION	ON-THE-JOB EXPERIENCE AT HOME	EXPOSURE TO OTHER CULTURES	BASIC EDUCATION
Maintain healthy devotional life, including prayer for world missions and God's direction. Keep quiet time journal. Be involved in small group or one-on-one discipleship for growth and accountability.	Begin to use and discover spiritual gifts. Involved in at least 2 areas of local ministry most applicable to field ministry interest. Lead a small group, discipleship, or Sunday school class. Seek opportunities to gain experience in chosen profession.	Consider short-term missions experience. Develop an international friendship. Interact with people who have lived in other cultures. Inner-city ministry.	Reading from Stage 1 and 2 book list. Attend CSPC's annual missions conference. Meet with missionaries on home assignment. Attend quarterly missionary training session. Attend one of committee's missionary interviews.

Phase 2: Getting There

AGENCY CONTACT AND CANDIDACY	MINISTRY ASSIGNMENT SEARCH	HANDS-ON MISSIONARY TRAINING
Assigned to a guidance group of missions committee and submit quarterly reports. Seek to determine what is involved in missionary service, whether qualified, confirm calling and role of church. Explore policies of missions agencies. Explore possible roles with several agencies.	Explore most appropriate roles with chosen agency. Consult with guidance communications and missions communications as to final placement. Continue to meet with care group who uphold you and your ministry through your term of service.	Complete agency's pre-field requirements and training. Complete any other training suggested by the missions communications and/or your guidance group, such as MTI's pre-field orientation (3 weeks).

Phase 3: Getting Established

APPRENTICESHIP/ INTERNSHIP	LIFELONG LEARNING	FINISHING STRONG
Dependiung upon candidate's work experience and ministry goal, a 2- to 3-year internship is recommended. Ex.: Work with a church planter in the U.S. as a paid intern or volunteer.	Many sending agencies provide opportunities for missionaries to sharpen their skills. For our own members, we assist financially in additional education costs.	We encourage missionaries to read *Too Valuable to Lose*, edited by William D. Taylor, so that they might explore the causes of attrition with the desire and plan that they will not be among the attrition statistics.

TRAINING PATH: HOPE CHAPEL (Austin, Texas)

Hope Chapel exists to persuade unconverted and unchurched individuals to come into a relationship with God through faith in Jesus Christ, and to incorporate/assimilate these individuals into God's family of relationships in the community of believers called Hope Chapel, so that they may grow in maturity, becoming like Jesus in every aspect of their lives, and be adequately equipped to serve to their maximum potential either in Hope Chapel or as one sent out from among us, in order to plant churches in unchurched neighborhoods and cities of the world, so that all the nations of the world may glorify God. Hope Chapel is committed to sending its members to serve on church planting teams in the unreached peoples and cities of the world.

Phase 1: Getting Ready

PERSONAL SPIRITUAL FORMATION

Assimilated into the life of the church and into a Hope Group for community, discipleship, and accountability.

ON-THE-JOB EXPERIENCE AT HOME

After active participation in a Hope Group, the candidate moves toward purposeful leadership development as a Hope Group intern then shepherd.

EXPOSURE TO OTHER CULTURES

Designed involvement with international students and short-term mission vision/ministry trips.

BASIC EDUCATION

Team members combine formal, non-formal, and informal educational modes for pre-field equipping. We encourage distance and residential study with a strong missions ethos and curriculum. Candidate stays closely linked to church life. Strategic access missionaries acquire professional requirements.

Phase 2: Getting There

AGENCY CONTACT AND CANDIDACY

We send members to serve on church planting teams in the unreached world; we will develop strategic alliances with existing mission agencies for field strategizing and support systems.

MINISTRY ASSIGNMENT SEARCH

Research done by mission candidates and leadership to seek right combination of philosophy of ministry, skill set, gift mix, and spiritual needs. Assignment after confirmation of the Spirit and leadership.

HANDS-ON MISSIONARY TRAINING

Overlap with educational modes, plus designed and evaluated ministry assignments. Pre-field orientation and language learning preparation prior to departure.

Phase 3: Getting Established

APPRENTICESHIP/ INTERNSHIP

Pre-field and on-field language study, contact, and team residence established with ministry context/people group.

LIFELONG LEARNING

We are committed to lifelong personal development program based on gifts, skills, and field needs. Periodic home assignment for renewal and study.

FINISHING STRONG

We are committed to ongoing evaluation and pastoral care, helping each missionary determine God's purpose, regardless of geography or ministry.

APPENDIX 2: GLOBAL MISSIONS RESOURCES FOR WORLD CHRISTIANS

Compiled by Dave Imboden, USCWM

Overview

There is an amazing array of ever-expanding resources to help you and your home church link effectively with global missions. Books, magazines, and videos are only the most obvious resources you can purchase or peruse to learn more. We have selected several of the most widely used agencies who supply the richest variety of books, magazines, and videos for World Christians. You will want to contact each of these organizations to receive their free catalogs.

Ministries to Help Your Church

ACMC (Advancing Churches in Missions Commitment). An interdenominational organization committed to helping local churches improve their missions programs by providing outstanding conferences and seminars across the U.S. They have also created excellent resources and guidebooks covering key issues churches face in doing missions. For more details, contact ACMC at 1-800-747-7346. Web: www.acmc.org.

AIMS (Accelerating International Mission Strategies). Helps renewal and charismatic churches connect with unreached peoples opportunities and provides various resources and seminars to train churches in missions involvement. For more details, contact: AIMS, P.O. Box 64534, Virginia Beach, VA 23464 Phone: 1-757-579-5850. E-mail: AIMS@cbn.org. Web: www.aims.org.

Brigada. Provides online missions resources and a weekly e-mail newsletter. Subscribe via e-mail: hub@xc.org with the following message: subscribe Brigada. Web: www.brigada.org.

Caleb Project. A mobilization agency providing unreached peoples videos, prayer guides, prayer cards, mission drama scripts, manuals on researching unreached people groups, brochures on miscellaneous mission topics, as well as primary ministry tracking with "people-specific advocates" (individuals promoting a specific unreached people for adoption among multiple churches). Contact: Caleb Project, 10 W. Dry Creek Circle, Littleton, CO 80120. Phone: 1-303-730-4170, ext. 343. E-mail: info@cproject.com. Web: www.calebproject.org.

U.S. Center for World Mission. Publishes *Mission Frontiers* and the *Global Prayer Digest*; facilitates the U.S. "Perspectives on the World Christian Movement" study program and the "World Christian Foundations" B.A. completion/M.A. degree programs. The USCWM also facilitates the global and U.S. Adopt-A-People Campaigns and provides various local church-oriented resources, such as the "Vision for the Nations" video-training curriculum, unreached peoples videos, and other AAP how-to resources. For more details, contact: USCWM, 1605 E. Elizabeth St., Pasadena, CA 91104. Phone: 1-626-398-2200. E-mail: USCWMmob@aol.com. Web: www.uscwm.org.

William Carey Library (at the USCWM) has the broadest list of mission titles available in the following categories: World Christian books, missionary biographies, World Christian periodicals, prayer resources, resources to ignite vision in your church, international students, listings of specialized training seminars, assistance to local churches, and ministries to help your church in missions. All books are available at discount prices (wholesale when 3 or more are purchased). For prices and ordering information call: 1-626-798-0819. Web: www.uscwm.org.

World Christian Foundations. WCF is the U.S. Center for World Mission's innovative B.A. completion or M.A. degree program. WCF is available from accredited colleges and can be taken in the field virtually anywhere in the world or on campus at the USCWM. Costs vary by school through which students register. Phone: 1-626-398-2106. E-mail: wcf@uscwm.org.

World Christian Periodicals

Echo. A new publication merging *VOX* and *Wherever* magazines. Published three times a year and distributed to 100,000 students and young adults through campuses, church ministries, and Christian events. Presents discipleship, worship, and missions involvement as a biblical model for the World Christian. Contact: VoxCorp, 2525-C Lebanon Pike, Nashville, TN 37214. Phone: 1-800-352-7225. E-mail: echo@echomagazine.com. Web: www.echomagazine.com.

Evangelical Missions Quarterly. Focused on missions in general, this practical publication for practitioners contains a wealth of material dealing with a wide variety of issues concerning the mission task. Includes book reviews and world news. Write: EMQ, P.O. Box 794, Wheaton, IL 60189. Subscription: $21.95 per year.

International Journal of Frontier Missions. The only scholarly journal focused solely on contemporary frontier missiology. A must for those seeking to keep abreast of the latest issues in finishing world evangelization. Write: IJFM, 7665 Wenda Way, El Paso, TX 79915. Phone: 1-915-775-2464. E-mail: 103121.2610@ compuserve.com. Subscription: 1 year (quarterly), $15.00; 2 years, $28.00.

MARC Newsletter. A free bimonthly information newsletter on missions research from the Missions Advanced Research and Communication Center (a division of World Vision International). Write: MARC Newsletter, 800 W. Chestnut Ave., Monrovia, CA 91016-3198. Phone: 1-800-777-7752. E-mail: MARC@wvi.org.

Mission Frontiers. An indispensable bimonthly bulletin (free subscription) highlighting key news, events, leaders, and ideas from the USCWM, Adopt-A-People, the AD 2000 and Beyond Movement, World Evangelical Fellowship, and other organizations promoting frontier mission and world evangelization. Write: MF/USCWM, 1605 E. Elizabeth St., Pasadena, CA 91104. Also available on the Web at: www.uscwm.org.

Pulse. An eight-page biweekly publication of world news, commentaries, and calendar of mission-related events; indispensable to stay current on world evangelization. Write: Pulse, P.O. Box 794, Wheaton, IL 60189. Phone: 1-630-653-2158. Subscription: $26.95 per year.

Prayer Resources

Global Prayer Digest. Monthly prayer devotional with breakthrough news of what God is doing around the world. Features an unreached people to pray for each day, as well as glimpses into other cultures. A daily mission-related Scripture verse and commentary, with an insightful article covering the target region being prayed for each month. Available in English, Spanish, Portuguese, and Korean. Contact GPD Subscriptions: 1-626-398-2249. Web: www.uscwm.org.

30-Day Prayer Focus. Booklets and videos that provide daily prayer for Muslims and Hindus. Issues on Buddhism and other religions planned. For more information or a catalog contact: World Christian News and Books, P.O. Box 26479, Colorado Springs, CO 80936. Phone: 1-719-442-6409. E-mail: wcn@xc.org.

Operation World. Patrick Johnstone. The mostly widely used day-by-day guide to praying for the world, deliberately designed as a prayer manual, highlighting facts and figures from over 220 nations to stimulate intercession. Grand Rapids: Zondervan, 1997. To order, call William Carey Library at 1-626-798-0819. Web: www.uscwm.org.

Personal Prayer Diary and Planner. One unreached people group, needy nation, or world class city is listed every day, with space to journal your prayers. Includes current world maps, statistics, sketches of people, details about the population, religion, percentage of known Christians, and more to fuel your intercession, as well as world time zones and information about Youth With a Mission. Contact YWAM Publishing, P.O. Box 55787, Seattle, WA 98155. Phone: 1-800-922-2143 (U.S. only) or 1-425-771-1153.

Strongholds of the 10/40 Window: Intercessors Guide to the World's Least Evangelized Nations. George Otis, Jr., Editor, with Mark Brockman. A handbook for those serious about prayer for global evangelism, especially within the 10/40 Window, which encloses almost 100% of the world's 1.1 billion Muslims, 800 million Hindus, and 300 million Buddhists. YWAM Publishing, 1995, paperback, 278 pp.

Worship and Warfare: A Prayer Companion. Richard Webster. A treasure of truths to vary and enrich your prayer ministry, whether alone or in a group. Names of God, reminders of His character, hymns, quotes, and Scripture verses will stimulate, guide, and refresh your prayer times. William Carey Library, 1993, 48 pp. Phone: 1-626-798-0819. Web: www.uscwm.org.

APPENDIX 3: MISSIONS TRAINING DIRECTORY
A LIST OF COLLEGES, SEMINARIES, AND SCHOOLS WITH A FOCUS ON MISSIONS

Schools in the United States

Assemblies of God Theological Seminary
1425 N. Glenstone
Springfield, MO 65802 USA
Phone: 1-800-467-AGTS
E-mail: agts@agseminary.edu
Web: www.agts.edu

Azusa Pacific University
Department of Global Studies
901 E. Alosta Ave.
Azusa, CA 91702 USA
Phone: 1-626-815-6000, ext. 3844
E-mail: rslimbach@apu.edu
Web: www.apu.edu

Beeson Divinity School
800 Lakeshore Dr.
Birmingham, AL 35229 USA
Phone: 1-800-888-8266
E-mail: wrobrien@samford.edu
Web: www.beeson.samford.edu

Bethany College of Missions
6820 Auto Club Rd.
Minneapolis, MN 55438 USA
Phone: 1-800-323-3417
E-mail: bcom@bethfel.org
Web: www.bcom.org

Biola University
School of International Studies
13800 Biola Ave.
La Mirada, CA 90639-0001 USA
Phone: 1-800-OKBIOLA
E-mail: admissions@biola.edu
Web: www.biola.edu

Christ for the Nations
P.O. Box 769000
Dallas, TX 75376-9000 USA
Phone: 1-214-376-1711
E-mail: missions@cfni.org
Web: www.cfni.org

Columbia International University
P.O. Box 3122
Columbia, SC 29203-3122 USA
(continued next column)

Phone: 1-800-777-2227
E-mail: yescbs@ciu.edu;
  bodonnel@ciu.edu
Web: www.ciu.edu

Dallas Theological Seminary
3909 Swiss Ave.
Dallas, TX 75204 USA
Phone: 1-800-992-0998
E-mail: external_studies@dts.edu
Web: www.dts.edu

Denver Seminary
P.O. Box 10000
Denver, CO 80250-0100 USA
Phone: 1-800-922-3040
E-mail: info@densem.edu
Web: www.gospelcom.net/densem/

Eastern Baptist Theological Seminary
6 Lancaster Ave.
Wynnewood, PA 19096 USA
Phone: 1-800-220-3287
E-mail: ewelles@ebts.edu;
  registrar@ebts.edu
Web: www.ebts.edu

Eastern College
10 Fairview Dr.
St. Davids, PA 19087 USA
Phone: 1-610-341-5972
E-mail: gradadm@eastern.edu
Web: www.eastern.edu

Fuller School of World Missions
135 N. Oakland Ave.
Pasadena, CA 91182 USA
Phone: 1-800-AFULLER
E-mail: admiss@fuller.edu
Web: www.fuller.edu

Gordon-Conwell Theological Seminary
130 Essex St.
South Hamilton, MA 01982 USA
Phone: 1-978-468-7111
Fax: 1-978-468-6691
E-mail: info@gcts.edu;
  adminfo@gcts.edu
Web: www.gcts.edu

Hope International University
2500 E. Nutwood Ave.
Fullerton, CA 92831 USA
Phone: 1-714-879-3903
E-mail: ejelliston@hiu.edu
Web: www.hiu.edu

Los Angeles Missionary Internship
3800 Canon Blvd.
Altadena, CA 98001 USA
Phone: 1-626-797-7903
E-mail: philelkins@aol.com

Mission Training International
P.O. Box 50110
Colorado Springs, CO 80949 USA
Phone: 1-800-896-3710
E-mail: mintern@aol.com
Web: www.mti.org

Moody Bible Institute
820 N. LaSalle Blvd.
Chicago, IL 60610 USA
Phone: 1-800-955-1123
E-mail: missions@moody.edu
Web: www.moody.edu

Multnomah Biblical Seminary
8435 N.E. Glisan St.
Portland, OR 97220 USA
Phone: 1-800-275-4672
E-mail: admiss@multnomah.edu
Web: www.multnomah.edu

New Tribes Mission
1000 E. First St.
Sanford, FL 32771 USA
Phone: 1-407-323-3430
E-mail: ntm@ntm.org
Web: www.ntm.org

Nyack College
1 South Blvd.
Nyack, NY 10960 USA
Phone: 1-800-33-NYACK
E-mail: enroll@nyack.edu;
  sinkeyw@nyack.edu
Web: www.nyackcollege.edu

Operation Mobilization
P.O. Box 444
Tyrone, GA 30290 USA
Phone: 1-770-631-0432
E-mail: info@omusa.om.org
Web: www.om.org

Reformed Theological Seminary
Jackson, FL; Orlando, FL;
Charlotte, NC USA
Phone: 1-800-227-2013
E-mail: rts@rts.edu
Web: www.rts.edu

Regent University
1000 Regent University Dr.
Virginia Beach, VA 23464 USA
Phone: 1-800-373-5504
E-mail: admissions@regent.edu
Web: www.regent.edu

School of Intercultural Learning
(at Western Seminary)
5511 S.E. Hawthorne Blvd.
Portland, OR 97215 USA
Phone: 1-800-547-4546
Fax: 1-503-239-4216
E-mail: dis@westernseminary.edu
Web: www.westernseminary.edu

The Stanway Institute
Trinity Episcopal School for Ministry
311 Eleventh St.
Ambridge, PA 15003 USA
Phone: 1-800-874-8754
E-mail: admissions@tesm.edu
Web: www.episcopalian.org/tesm

Trinity Evangelical Divinity School
2065 Half Day Rd.
Deerfield, IL 60015 USA
Phone: 1-800-345-TEDS
E-mail: tedsadm@tiu.edu
Web: www.tiu.edu/teds/

U.S. Center for World Mission
Training Division
1605 E. Elizabeth St.
Pasadena, CA 91104 USA
Phone: 1-626-398-2510
Fax: 1-626-398-2111
E-mail: training@uscwm.org
Web: www.uscwm.org

University of the Nations (YWAM)
P.O. Box 7736
Richmond, VA 23231 USA
Phone: 1-804-222-4013
Fax: 1-804-236-8896
E-mail: haystack@haystack.org
Web: www.haystack.org

Wheaton Graduate School
Missions Department
Wheaton College
Wheaton, IL 60187 USA
Phone: 1-800-888-0141
Fax: 1-630-752-5935
E-mail: gradadm@wheaton.edu
Web: www.wheaton.edu

William Carey International University
1539 E. Howard St.
Pasadena, CA 91104 USA
Phone: 1-626-398-2141
Fax: 1-626-398-2111
E-mail: registrar@wciu.edu
Web: www.wciu.edu

Worldwide Evangelization for Christ (WEC)
P.O. Box 1707
Fort Washington, PA 19034 USA
Phone: 1-215-646-2322
Fax: 1-215-646-6202
E-mail: 76145.1774@compuserve.com
Web: www.cin.co.uk/wec

Wycliffe Bible Translators (SIL)
7500 W. Camp Wisdom Rd.
Dallas, TX 75236-5699 USA
Phone: 1-800-892-3356
Fax: 1-972-708-7380
E-mail: sil_adm@sil.org
Web: www.sil.org

Schools in Canada

ACTS (Associated Canadian Theological Schools of Trinity Western University)
7600 Glover Rd.
Langley, British Columbia V2Y 1Y1
CANADA
Phone: 1-888-687-2287
Fax: 1-604-513-2045
E-mail: acts@twu.ca
Web: www.acts.twu.ca

Briercrest Biblical Seminary
510 College Dr.
Carenport, Saskatchewan S0H 0S0
CANADA
Phone: 1-800-667-5199
E-mail: jsills@briercrest.ca
Web: www.briercrest.ca

Canada Institute of Linguistics
7600 Glover Rd.
Langley, British Columbia V2Y 1Y1
CANADA
Phone: 1-604-888-6124
Fax: 1-604-888-4617
E-mail: caniladmissions@twu.ca
Web: www.canil.twu.ca

Gateway: Training for Cross-Cultural Service
21233 32nd Ave.
Langley, British Columbia V2Z 2E7
CANADA
Phone: 1-604-530-3252
Fax: 1-604-530-3252
E-mail: 74151.3437@compuserve.com
Web: www.gatewaytraining.org

Prairie Bible College
P.O. Box 4000
Three Hills, Alberta T0M 2N0
CANADA
Phone: 1-800-785-4226
Fax: 1-403-443-5540
E-mail: distance.ed@pbi.ab.ca
Web: www.pbi.ab.ca

Prairie Graduate School
2540 5th Ave. N.W.
Calgary, Alberta T2N 0T5
CANADA
Phone: 1-800-239-0422
E-mail: gradschool.admissions@pbi.ab.ca;
    distance.ed@pbi.ab.ca
Web: www.pbi.ab.ca

Providence Theological Seminary
Otterburne, Manitoba R0A 1G0
CANADA
Phone: 1-800-668-7768
Fax: 1-204-433-7158
E-mail: info@providence.mb.ca
Web: www.providence.mb.ca

Regent College
5800 University Blvd.
Vancouver, BC V6T 2E4
CANADA
Phone: 1-800-663-8664
Fax: 1-604-224-3097
E-mail: admissions@regent-college.edu
Web: www.regent-college.edu

Tyndale College and Seminary
25 Ballyconnor Ct.
Toronto, Ontario M2M 4B3
CANADA
Phone: 1-800-663-6052
Fax: 1-416-663-6052
E-mail: info@tyndale-canada.edu
Web: www.tyndale-canada.edu

Schools in the United Kingdom

All Nations Christian College
Easneye, Ware, Herts SG12 8LX
UNITED KINGDOM
Phone: 01920 461243
Fax: 01920 462997
E-mail: mailbox@allnations.ac.uk

Belfast Bible College
Glenburne House
Glenburn Road South
Dunmurry, Belfast BT17 PJP
UNITED KINGDOM
Phone: 01232 301551
Fax: 01232 431758
E-mail: staff@bbc.dnet.co.uk

Glasgow Bible College
731 Great Western Rd.
Glasgow G12 8QX
UNITED KINGDOM
Phone: 0141 334 9849
Fax: 0141 334 0012

London Bible College
Green Lane
Northwood, Middlx HA6 2UW
UNITED KINGDOM
Phone: 01923 826061
Fax: 01923 836530
E-mail: lbc@mailbox.ulcc.ac.uk

Moorlands College
Sopley
Christchurch, Dorset BH23 7AT
UNITED KINGDOM
Phone: 01425 672369
Fax: 01425 674162
E-mail: Moorlands_College@cin.co.uk.internet

Oxford Centre for Mission Studies
P.O. Box 70
Oxford, Oxon OX2 6HB
UNITED KINGDOM
Phone: 01865 556071
Fax: 01865 510823
E-mail: ocms@xc.org; 100270.2155@compuserve.com

Redcliffe College
Wotton House
Horton Road, Gloucester GL1 3PT
UNITED KINGDOM
Phone: 01452 308097
Fax: 01452 503949
E-mail: Redcliffe_College@cin.co.uk

St. John's Extension Studies
Bramcote
Nottingham, Notts NG9 3RL
UNITED KINGDOM
Phone: 0115 925 1117
Fax: 0115 943 6438

Trinity College
Stoke Hill
Bristol, Avon BS9 1JP
UNITED KINGDOM
Phone: 0117 96828803
Fax: 0117 9687470
E-mail: howard.peskett@bristol.ac.uk

Schools in the Netherlands

Amsterdam GateWay (YWAM)
Kadijksplein 18 1018 AC
Amsterdam, THE NETHERLANDS
Phone: 31-20-6279536
Fax: 31-20-6221451
E-mail: ywamadam@xs4all.nl
Web:www.xs4all.nl/~ywamadam/YWAM/Amsterdam/

APPENDIX 4:
GLOBAL WWW RESOURCES: GLOBAL MISSIONS AT YOUR FINGERTIPS

There is a multitude of information about missions now available on the World Wide Web. Below we have listed resources on the Web as well as some other resources which will help you in finding your way in missions, from missions organizations to information on unreached people groups.

If you are interested in updates on what new is happening on the Web and additional Web resources, we recommend looking into *Evangelical Missions Quarterly*. Scott Moreau of Wheaton Graduate School and Mike O'Rear, president of Global Missions International, are heading a department in EMQ entitled "Missions on the Web." This is an excellent resource. They both also have Web sites which are excellent starting points in your search of the Web. Look for Scott Moreau at www.wheaton.edu/Missions/Moreau, and Mike O'Rear at www.gmi.org.

Search Engines

Search engines are computer programs that look through the texts of Web pages that have been registered in databases. Each search engine has its own database, so it is often good and necessary to utilize several search engines in a single search. If you do not find what you need on the first search engine, looking on another one could yield better results. Below are several search engines you can try:

AltaVista	http://altavista.digital.com
Excite	http://my.excite.com/help
HotBot	www.hotbot.com
Infoseek	www2.infoseek.com
LookSmart	www.looksmart.com
Lycos	www.lycos.com
Mining Co.	http://home.miningco.com
Net Search	www.search.com
Northern Light	www.nilsearch.com
Metacrawler	www.metacrawler.com
Yahoo!	www.yahoo.com

Metacrawler is one of the best search engines because it compiles data from several other search engines, including AltaVista, Excite, Infoseek, Lycos, Web Crawler, and Yahoo! For an Internet listing of all these searches and more, see www.gmi.org/research/search.htm.

General Missions Information

The Christian Information Network
11205 State Highway 83
Colorado Springs, CO 80921 USA
Phone: 1-888-772-9104; 1-719-522-1040
Fax: 1-719-548-9000
E-mail: cin10_40@compuserve.com
Web: www.Christian-info.com

Christianity.net
Web: www3.christianity.net:81
A search engine covering *Christianity Today*'s database of 3,000 Christian resources, and more.

Cross Connect
P.O. Box 70632
Seattle, WA 98107 USA
Phone: 1-206-781-0461; Fax: 1-206-781-0571
E-mail: info@xc.org
Web: www.xc.org

DAWN
Web: www.jesus.org.uk/dawn
A missions news service.

Ethnologue
Web: www.sil.org/ethnologue/ethnologue.html
A catalog of the world's languages, including sociolinguistic and demographic information.

Fields International
Web: www.fields.org
Contains worldwide missions news, as well as a comprehensive table of missions organizations with connections to their respective Web sites.

Fingertip
Web: www.globalmission.org/fingertip.htm
Offers a variety of services, ranging from mission news to listings of mission agencies to a searchable database of job listings with missions agencies.

Global Evangelization Movement
P.O. Box 6628
Richmond, VA 23230 USA
Phone: 1-804-355-1646; Fax: 1-804-355-2016
E-mail: JustinLong@xc.org
Web: www.gem-werc.org

Lausanne Committee for World Evangelization (LCWE)
E-mail: Lausanne@powertech.no
Web: http://goshen.net/Lausanne

MAF
Web: www.xc.org/cgi-bin/serverlist.cgi
Host for a number of missions' and Christian organizations' Web pages as well as individually tailored missions oriented e-mail conferences.

Missiology Resource Guide
Web: www.missiology.net
A guide to resources concerning the study of missions.

Mission America
Web: www.missionamerica.org
A coalition of over 300 North American Christian leaders working in conjunction with AD 2000.

Mission Resource Directory
Web: www.xc.org/helpintl/mrd.htm
A place to start your search; lists of missions resources.

Morningstar Resources
Web: www.morningstar.org/world-christian.html

Missions Opportunities Information

Global Missions Event Calendar
Web: www.globalmission.org/calendar.htm

SIM
Web: www.sim.org
Lists Protestant mission agency Web sites in four categories: traditional missions, relief missions, mission research and support, and denominational missions.

Summer Institute of Linguistics
Web: www.sil.org
Helps and links to other Web sites in the academic areas of linguistics, anthropology, literacy, language learning, translation, and computing.

Wycliffe Bible Translators
Web: www.wycliffe.org
Information about Wycliffe's translation work and opportunities.

YWAM (Youth With a Mission)
Web: www.ywam.org
Information about YWAM's various ministries and educational opportunities.

Unreached People Groups and Unevangelized World

Accelerating International Mission Strategies
Web: www.aims.org
A resource for aligning and uniting the church to reach the unreached peoples of the world.

AD 2000 and Beyond Movement
2860 South Circle Dr., Suite 2112
Colorado Springs, CO 80906 USA
Phone: 1-719-576-2000; Fax: 1-719-576-2685
E-mail: info@ad2000.org
Web: www.ad2000.org

Adopt-A-People Campaign
USCWM
1605 E. Elizabeth St.
Pasadena, CA 91104 USA
Phone: 1-818-398-2200
E-mail: aap.campaign@wciu.edu

Brigada
Web: www.brigada.org
A system of conferences and forums that allows you to network with others who share common interests in sharing God's love with previously unreached cities and peoples around the world.

Brigada/Team Expansion
3700 Hopewell Rd.
Louisville, KY 40299-5002 USA
Phone: 1-502-297-0006; Fax: 1-502-297-9823
E-mail: teamexpansion@xc.org
Web: www.teamexpansion.org

CAC (Creative Access Convention)
E-mail: cac@spidernet.com.cy

Caleb Project
10 W. Dry Creek Circle
Littleton, CO 80120 USA
Phone: 1-303-730-4170; Fax: 1-303-730-4177
E-mail: info@cproject.com
Web: www.calebproject.org
Provides information on connections with the 10/40 Window, missions opportunities, and prayer guides focused on unreached peoples.

The Christian Information Network
11205 State Highway 83
Colorado Springs, CO 80921 USA
Phone: 1-888-772-9104; 1-719-522-1040
Fax: 1-719-548-9000
E-mail: cin10_40@compuserve.com
Web: www.Christian-info.com

Global Harvest Ministries
P.O. Box 63060
Colorado Springs, CO 80962-3060 USA
Phone: 1-719-262-9922; Fax: 1-719-262-9920
E-mail: 74114.570@compuserve.com

Joshua Project 2000 Peoples List
3806 Monument Ave.
Richmond, VA 23230 USA
Fax: 1-804-254-8980
E-mail: 753-8054@mcimail.com
Web: www.ad2000.org/Peoples/index.htm

World Mission Centre
P.O. Box 36147
Menlo Park 0102
Pretoria, SOUTH AFRICA
Phone: 012-343-1165
Fax: 012-343-1167
E-mail: wmcentre@cis.co.za
Web: www.worldmissioncentre.co.za

Bivocational/Tentmaking Information Resources

INTENT
(Formerly U.S. Association of Tentmakers or USAT)
P.O. Box 35
Cascade, CO 80809 USA
Phone: 1-719-471-6600
Fax: 1-719-684-9391

SIM TEC
Web: http://soter.houghton.edu/simtec
A Christian computer training missions project organized by SIM, to equip people to minister Christ through computer education in the unevangelized world.

Tentmaker International Exchange (TIE)
P.O. Box 45880
Seattle, WA 98145-0880 USA
Phone: 1-206-524-4600
Fax: 1-206-524-6992
E-mail: tie@gati.wa.com

Tentmakers Speak: Practical Advice From Over 400 Missionary Tentmakers
Don Hamilton, 1987
TMQ Research
32 Melcanyon Rd.
Duarte, CA 91010 USA
Phone: 1-818-303-5533

Working Your Way to the Nations: A Guide to Effective Tentmaking
Jonathan Lewis, Editor, 1996
InterVarsity Press

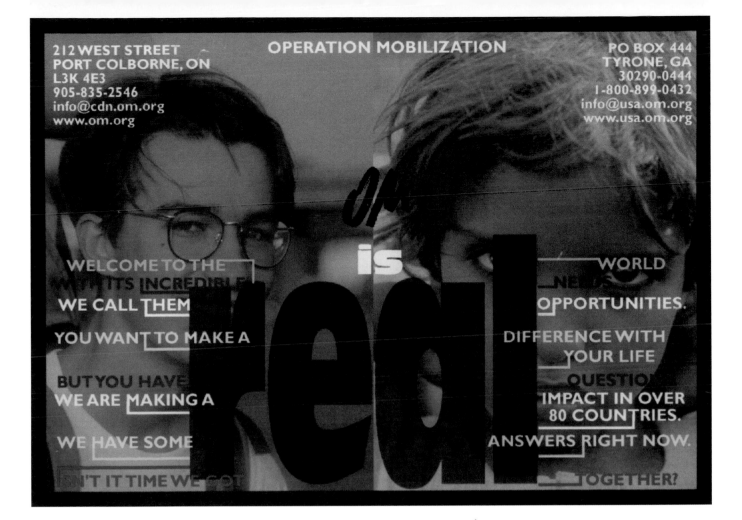

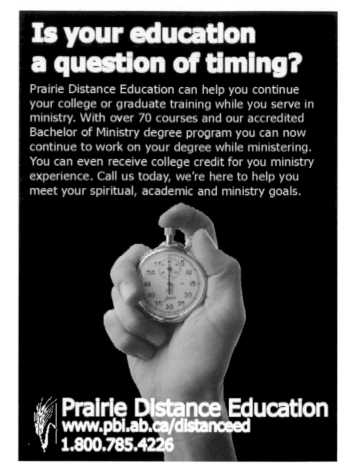
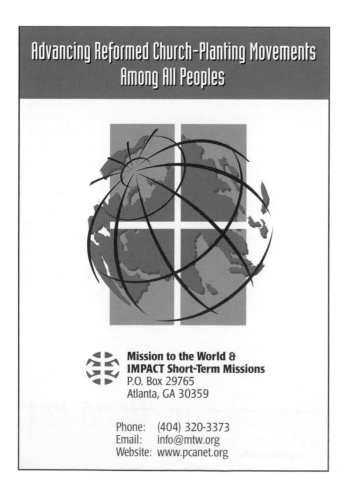
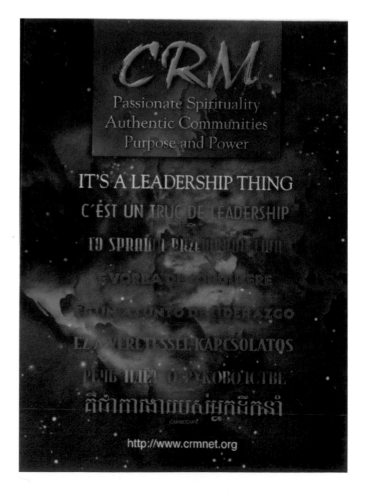

Her people need Jesus

Do you have a clear picture?

Oh, India!

Get It!

www.missionfrontiers.org

Mission Frontiers is a bimonthly magazine of the U.S. Center for World Mission. Subscriptions are by donation but available free upon request. To subscribe, see our web site, E-mail us at <mission.frontiers@uscwm.org>, call (626) 398-2249, or write us at: Mission Frontiers Subscriptions, 1605 E. Elizabeth St. Pasadena CA 91104.